BRIGHT NOTES

WHO'S AFRAID OF VIRGINIA WOOLF? AND OTHER WORKS BY EDWARD ALBEE

Intelligent Education

Nashville, Tennessee

BRIGHT NOTES: Who's Afraid of Virginia Woolf? and Other Works

www.BrightNotes.com

No part of this publication may be used or reproduced in any manner whatsoever without written permission, except in the case of brief quotations in critical articles and reviews. For permissions, contact Influence Publishers http://www.influencepublishers.com.

ISBN: 978-1-645420-94-1 (Paperback)
ISBN: 978-1-645420-95-8 (eBook)

Published in accordance with the U.S. Copyright Office Orphan Works and Mass Digitization report of the register of copyrights, June 2015.

Originally published by Monarch Press.
Michael Stugrin, 1972
2020 Edition published by Influence Publishers.

Interior design by Lapiz Digital Services. Cover Design by Thinkpen Designs.

Printed in the United States of America.

Library of Congress Cataloging-in-Publication Data forthcoming.
Names: Intelligent Education
Title: BRIGHT NOTES: Who's Afraid of Virginia Woolf? and Other Works
Subject: STU004000 STUDY AIDS / Book Notes

CONTENTS

1) Introduction to Edward Albee — 1

2) The Zoo Story — 23

3) The Sandbox — 27

4) Fam and Yam — 30

5) The Death of Bessie Smith — 32

6) The American Dream — 37

7) Introduction to Who's Afraid of Virginia Woolf? — 42

8) The Ballad of the Sad Café — 44

9) Tiny Alice — 49

10) Malcolm — 54

11) A Delicate Balance — 57

12) Everything in the Garden — 64

13)	Box-Mao-Box	66
14)	All Over	74
15)	Critical Analysis of Who's Afraid of Virginia Woolf?	79
16)	Textual Analysis	82
	Act One: Fun and Games	82
	Act Two: Walpurgisnacht	87
	Act Three: The Exorcism	92
17)	Character Analysis	95
18)	The Meaning of Who's Afraid of Virginia Woolf?	108
19)	Essay Questions and Answers	120
20)	Bibliography	127

INTRODUCTION TO EDWARD ALBEE

BIOGRAPHICAL SKETCH

Edward Albee was born in Washington, D.C. on March 12, 1928. At the age of two weeks he was adopted by Reed and Frances Albee and taken to live in the family home in Westchester, New York. Albee's new father had inherited a nationwide chain of vaudeville theaters, the Keith-Albee Circuit, which had been founded by Edward Franklin Albee II. Though the enterprise was eventually sold, the family's show business acquaintances meant that young Albee was often exposed to theater personalities. Reed Albee died on August 2, 1961 and his obituary listed one other adopted child besides Edward, but to our knowledge Albee has never mentioned him in any interview.

Albee's childhood, to say the least, was extremely comfortable. A magazine reports that this was a time "of servants, tutors, riding lessons; winters in Miami, summers sailing on the Sound; there was a Rolls to bring him, smuggled in lap robes, to matinees in the city; an inexhaustible wardrobe housed in a closet big as a room..." ("Who Isn't Afraid of Edward Albee?" *Show*, February 1963, p. 83). Albee has never made any explicit comments about the happiness of his childhood. His father was believed, however, to be dominated by his wife, who was considerably younger than her husband and an avid athlete.

Albee was apparently very close to his maternal grandmother to whom he dedicated his short play, *The Sandbox*.

Albee's educational background is extremely erratic and marked by poor performance. Because his family spent many of their winters in Florida, Albee was often transferred from school to school and thus was unable to make many strong friendship ties. In a period of five years he was dismissed from three schools. He attended Rye Country Day School until he was eleven and then Lawrenceville, a preparatory school in New Jersey, beginning in 1940. He did poorly in his academic studies, and was asked to leave in 1943. Albee then spent a year at the Valley Forge Military Academy because his mother felt his poor performance would be remedied by strict discipline; the experiment was unsuccessful, and he left there and entered the Choate School at Wallingford, Connecticut in 1944.

The two years at Choate were happy and productive ones for Albee. He began to read widely. During this period he published nine poems, eleven short stories, an essay on Johann Strauss, Jr., and a one-act play called *Schism* in the *Choate Literary Magazine*. While these pieces are imitative and trite, they nevertheless demonstrate an impressive facility with language and a sound sense of dialogue. On graduating from Choate in 1946, Albee enrolled at Trinity College, a small liberal arts institution in Hartford, Connecticut. Although his stay there was brief, he gained some dramatic experience playing the role of Emperor Franz Joseph in Maxwell Anderson's *The Masque of Kings*. This stay at Trinity was the final **episode** in his formal education, except for brief enrollments at Washington University and Columbia.

Albee left his parents' home in 1950, expressing a strong desire to become a writer. With the assistance of a fifty-dollar per week income from a trust-fund established by his grandmother in 1949 and a variety of part-time jobs, he was able to set up an apartment in Greenwich Village. His part-time jobs in this period from his twenty-first to his thirtieth birthday included working as an office-boy in an advertising agency, writing music programs for a radio station, selling records at Bloomingdale's and books at Gimbel's, and running messages for Western Union.

During this long period he worked at his writing continuously, yet the results of these efforts are largely unknown. With the exception of a single poem published in a Texas literary journal, the poetry he wrote and a long novel have never been made available for study. We do know, however, that his roommate during part of this time was a young composer, William Flanagan, who later wrote the music for *The Sandbox* and *Malcolm*, and a musical adaptation, *Billy Budd*. Flanagan has given us some knowledge of the writers who influenced Albee during this period of development - Tennessee Williams and Samuel Beckett, for example, were among Albee's literary heroes. Albee also met W. H. Auden, who suggested that he develop his art by writing pornographic verse; and in 1953 he met Thornton Wilder at the MacDowell Colony in Peterborough, New Hampshire, who suggested that he concentrate on drama.

It was a rather dramatic event when, nearly on the eve of his thirtieth birthday, Albee sat down and wrote his first major play, *The Zoo Story*, which was first produced in 1959. From this point on Albee began to establish himself as a major figure in the American theater. After helping to establish a genuine avant-garde movement, he entered the ranks of Broadway playwrights in 1962 with his most famous play, *Who's Afraid of Virginia Woolf?*

For over a decade Albee has regularly introduced plays on the American stage - to this date he has written thirteen plays.

He is a noteworthy figure in the American theater not only for his works, but also for his efforts to introduce new talent and techniques. In 1962 Albee and two young producers, Richard Barr and Clinton Wilder, founded the Cherry Lane Theater, which in its first year produced nine plays, all in the Absurdist tradition. Among them were his own plays, *The Zoo Story* and *The American Dream*; also, Jean Genet's *Deathwatch*, Eugene Ionesco's *The Killer*, and Samuel Beckett's *Endgame*. Two years later, the three men founded "Theater 1964" which funded such plays as Beckett's *Play* and Pinter's *The Lover*. Since then Albee has helped to found the Playwright's Unit which has received substantial grants from the Rockefeller Foundation and the New York State Council of the Arts. This organization produced over a hundred plays, but at the present time, the Unit is dormant and Albee is engaged in still another project to sponsor creative literary efforts - the William Flanagan Center for Creative Persons, which is funded solely by Albee with the world-wide profits derived from *The American Dream* and *The Zoo Story*. Called "The Stable" by its inhabitants, it is located on a property Albee purchased in 1969 at Montauk, Long Island.

In addition to his writing and his efforts in sponsoring new plays, Albee has participated in a wide variety of symposiums on drama and the arts and has lectured to college audiences throughout the country. In 1963 he spent a month in the Soviet Union on a tour sponsored by the American State Department. The awards Albee has received for his work have been quite impressive, especially the Pulitzer Prize, which he received in 1967 for *A Delicate Balance*.

At the present time Albee is working on several plays, including a longstanding project called "The Substitute Speaker". Another play, *Seascape*, is supposed to be produced on Broadway soon: Albee has said that it is a companion piece of *All Over* and that the two will carry the joint title *Life and Death*.

ALBEE'S PHILOSOPHY AND ARTISTRY

In an interview in 1946 Eugene O'Neill commented on something his father had said: "'The theater is dying.' And those words seem to me as true today as when he said them. But the theater must be a hardy wench, for although she is still ailing, she will never die as long as she offers an escape." O'Neill's statement seems particularly relevant to this discussion of Albee's philosophical and artistic beliefs and to the analysis of *Who's Afraid of Virginia Woolf?* which follows in the next chapter. First of all, the statement reveals that O'Neill felt much the same way about the state of the theater in his day as Albee feels about the theater today - that it is ailing though its function in society is still an important one. Second, it capsulizes the dichotomy between the two playwrights' convictions about what the theater should offer to the public. Third, it serves as a cogent reminder that despite the contributions which both O'Neill and Albee and many other playwrights have made, the theater still ails and will no doubt always be lacking in perfection.

The following discussion is meant to provide an awareness of the major philosophical and artistic premises of Edward Albee's work which either suggest themselves when we study the plays or which have been offered by Albee himself in the public media. Equipped with these insights we can attempt a detailed analysis of *Who's Afraid of Virginia Woolf?*

Is Albee a member of the Theater of the Absurd? What is the nature of his relationship with that movement? What are the major premises of his drama? What are the major **themes** and artistic qualities of his plays? Can one identify a continuity of **theme** and artistry running throughout the works? Why is Albee so very angry? What is the nature of his social commitment?

ALBEE AND THE THEATER OF THE ABSURD

One of the major contributions Albee has made is his important work in the introduction of the European Theater of the Absurd to the American theater. The beginning of his career in 1960 came at a time when the American theater was generally in decline; only on the college campuses was there a strong interest in new and innovative drama. Virtually unaware of the European avant-garde movement, professional theater had become reliant on the largely uncontroversial works of a handful of famous playwrights who had ceased to break ground years before and who had now discovered the pulse of popular idiom. It was primarily a naturalistic theater which combined a few shocking scenes, snatches of suspense, and an affirmation of existing values. The Theater Establishment situated on Broadway had in almost every respect oriented its values toward judging the worth of a play on the basis of box office returns. It was economically unfeasible, given such a clime, for a true American avant-garde movement to flourish - two such organizations, The Artist's Theater and The Living Theater, attempted to sustain such an outlet for new work, but both were forced to close because they lacked sufficient public support. Without such non-commercially oriented institutions operating in the dramatic community, large-scale experimentation is impossible.

In an article which Albee wrote for *The New York Times* (February 25, 1962), "Which Theater is the Absurd One?," he noted that in major European cities there were more numerous productions of the works of Absurdist playwrights - Adamov, Genet, Brecht, Beckett, Pinter, etc. - and the audiences seemed far more receptive and willing to support this exciting postwar movement. Even in Buenos Aires, he had discovered, there were over a hundred experimental theaters.

Albee's arrival on the American theater scene with *The Zoo Story* in 1960 and *The American Dream* in 1961 thus came at a time when conditions were ripe and, indeed, when there was a clear need for a new theater which did not offer merely an affirmation of public values and accommodation to financial backers. Thus along with Jack Gelber (*The Connection*, 1959), Kenneth Brown (*The Brig*, 1963), Arthur Kopit (*Oh Dad, Poor Dad*, 1960) and several other young playwrights, Albee introduced a drama which was directly inspired by the **themes** and techniques of the Theater of the Absurd, but which was adapted to an American idiom.

IS ALBEE AN ABSURDIST?

The artistic and philosophical relationship between Albee's drama and the Theater of the Absurd has been commonly misunderstood even though plays like *Who's Afraid of Virginia Woolf?* and *All Over* have come a long way from *The American Dream*. The original endorsement Albee gave of the Theater of the Absurd was based both on its refreshing technical innovations and on what he defined as its basic purpose: "to make a man face up to the human condition as it really is..." Albee has taken this as the basis for his drama - in every play and through every technical experiment he has remained essentially faithful to that premise. But in what significant ways does Albee differ from the Absurdists? In exploring this question, it would be helpful to briefly describe the major characteristics of the Theater of the Absurd and then to suggest the major points of departure.

The voices of Albee, Gelber, Pinter, and the entire Theater of the Absurd have been collectively called an "existential revolt" or, in the words of Camus, "a **metaphysical** rebellion" against the state of man in the universe. The impetus which gave rise to this re-examination of man's **metaphysical** state and subsequent revolt was the spectre of what T. S. Eliot called "The Waste Land" which is by now familiar to most students. It is a world of "broken images," of the destruction and sterility of war, of the alienation of man in a world which has become unintelligibly complex, of the impossibly difficult task of maintaining one's individuality and consciousness, and of the haunting possibility that God is dead. For people living in this "Waste Land," life is nothing but "Birth and copulation and death" and the bleak awareness of their own nonessentiality - thus of the meaninglessness and absurdity of existence. The pervasive feeling of Absurdity was defined by Camus in *The Myth of Sisyphus* as arising in the modern world when traditional illusions and firm, popularly relied upon truths of former times become almost comically irrelevant to a civilization decimated by war and alienated by a huge industrial machine. Consequently, man became dissociated from his place in the universe and became an exile who was separated from his own life - this awareness constitutes the feeling the Absurdity. The emergence of the Theater of the Absurd after the war became the literary expression of this new awareness of man's position in the universe, while Existentialism was adopted as its philosophical expression. These artists sought to demonstrate this awareness of man's alienation, his spiritual decay and sterility, his inertia and his horror at the spectre of death - in sum, "to make a man face up to the human condition as it really is..." This avant-garde movement thus seeks to expose the most terrible and despairing truths of man's existence; its techniques are typically wild and macabre, making full use of incongruity and ambiguity - familiar dramatic **conventions** could not express its subject matter. The world of the Absurd, in effect, is "flying apart" and man is actually decaying and being overcome with the overpowering nothingness of existence.

What, then, are the scenes of modern man and his world in the Theater of the Absurd? Since "nothing connects with nothing" in "The Waste Land," there is no reason why mushrooms cannot sprout in the dining room or that the entire stage should not collapse in Ionesco's *Amedee* and *The Future is in Eggs*. The mysterious knock at the door is the haunting presence of Pereira, the symbol of Death and subsequent Nothingness of the afterlife, in Eliot's *Sweeney Agonistes*; and the equally as mysterious arrival of Goldberg and McCann in Pinter's *The Birthday Party* takes Stanley into imminent darkness. The same spectre appears again in Ionesco's *The Chairs* in which the emptiness of the chairs drives the old couple to jump from the tower rather than to wait for death. There is also total inertia, the inability to act for oneself - Gogo and Didi in Beckett's *Waiting for Godot* announce their intention to leave, but remain motionless; and in his *Endgame* Nell and Meg, having no arms or legs, live in ash cans. All of these scenes are ones of desolation and despair in which decay is irreversible.

DEPARTURE FROM THE ABSURD

Albee's departure from this vision of man in the modern world is a significant one. The crucial difference between what we have seen in this philosophy of the abnegation of human existence and the position Albee takes is that he still retains a fundamental faith in man. While the true participants in the "**metaphysical rebellion**" see man existing in a state of exhaustion and disillusionment which makes him unable to act, Albee finds man living in a corrupt and unhappy world but as still possessing the ability to act and to function as a human being. Such assertive action can bring his salvation from an existence of absurdity and despair, though it may demand a high price. In *The Zoo Story, The Death of Bessie Smith, Who's Afraid of Virginia Woolf?* and throughout Albee's work, the anguish of the characters existing in their cliched, tormented social relationships is caused by the same kind of spiritual sickness and decay as that which infects the characters of Beckett's *Endgame* or Eliot's *Sweeney Agonistes*. Albee's characters are victims of this same state and they face the same spectre of alienation and nothingness. This fundamental decay, however, is not necessarily terminal (although it certainly can be), nor have Albee's characters become subhuman - they have not been created for the sole purpose of exhibiting spiritual malaise and inertia. Rather, their essential failure lies in a deep reluctance to face the reality of their human condition and of the incoherent and irrational universe. As defense mechanisms they have created their own private, self-isolating illusions and have participated in the many illusions which society sustains - such evasion and self-deception has caused a massive failure of communication and love. Thus, as the plays demonstrate, Albee's people are very lonely.

The illusions under which man lives, in Albee's view, become so fully integrated into his life that a differentiation between illusion and reality becomes a major problem. Like Brother Julian in *Tiny Alice*, man can become a pitiable, though well-intentioned victim in yielding to the attraction of comfort-giving illusion. In Julian's case, religious escapism is a viable alternative to the threat of losing the emotional security which an unquestioned belief in the Ineffable offers. But Albee considers that anything which provides a shield from the reality of the human condition is ultimately destructive. Though in dying Julian takes on the appearance of an heroic Christ-figure, he is clearly not admirable because he has never been able to define the boundary between believing and the need to believe, between what appeared to be the Divinity and how he wished it to appear. *Tiny Alice* is so significant because it emphatically demonstrates the consequences of not facing reality; Julian's life is a tragic waste, but an inevitable one.

Further, in dramatizing the state of man in the modern world, Albee does not show us characters who are overcome with the sense of Nothingness and who are waiting for the inevitable figure of death to knock at their door. Nor does their only hope of finding some kind of intelligible meaning in the universe necessitate an acceptance of their own Nothingness. Rather, Albee begins at a point in their lives when they are functioning, but when the signs of encroaching decay and spiritual nullity are first perceived. In the case of Harry and Edna in *A Delicate Balance*, for example, the night brings these spectres into closer proximity. In seeking shelter with Tobias and Agnes, the frightened couple discover their friends are infected with the same fear and their arrival only brings it into the open. But in the case of Tobias and Agnes, there is a confrontation with both this fear and their protective isolation. What emerges as the message of the play is that there can be no survival without human contact and love and that a house which has become a refuge from reality makes itself vulnerable to an encompassing madness. There is hope, however, that when fear comes again, Tobias and Agnes will be able to rely on each other and lend support to anyone else who is in the same position - there is thus no finality implied in the play, but only a clear presentation of the danger and the weapon which must be used against it.

A THEATER OF CONFRONTATION

In viewing man's condition in the universe, Albee is well aware of the changes which have occurred to turn that universe into a physical and spiritual wasteland. One might generalize in saying that there are two main aspects of Albee's desire to bring this awareness to American society: Rather than either accepting the necessity of illusion to ensure one's sanity or revolting from that despairing awareness and simply presenting a picture of desolation, Albee chooses to confront reality in his drama; and secondly, it is through this confrontation that he displays an abiding social commitment in which he seeks to make the theater not only relevant to the needs of society, but to make it a corrective force.

The Theater of Confrontation, a term coined by C.W.E. Bigsby, is meant in this discussion both to describe what Albee attempts to do in every play - to present his audience with a realistic, truthful picture of man and society, and in a more specific sense to describe a clearly defined process of confronting man with the truths of his existence and ending the illusions which bar him from communion with others. Such a process constitutes the action and purpose of *Who's Afraid of Virginia Woolf?*

TARGETS OF CONFRONTATION

What are the barriers which shield man from an awareness of his human condition? Where do they originate? The confrontation which Albee dramatizes is ultimately an extremely personal one in which the individual must come to an awareness of self. The illusions and self-deceits in which man finds refuge from reality and thus isolates himself can be a wide variety of things - the child which lives in the household of George and Martha in *Who's Afraid of Virginia Woolf?*, or the great institutions of society, such as organized religion or a false nationalistic or regionalistic pride (the myth of Southern elegance, for example). They can also be a sense of false well-being or naive optimism which places an untempered faith in the abilities of man. But most prevalent of all these illusions are the cliched family relationships which are sustained by social **convention** or merely habit, and which have become soured and void of affection. All of these illusions and many others similar to them are evasions from and actually products of "The Waste Land." (See our discussion of this term.) The task Albee sets out to accomplish is to destroy these illusions and build anew, or at least to make an individual acknowledge them for what they are. If any hope of salvation does exist in the world, it rests in man's own courage to save himself.

THE PROCESS OF CONFRONTATION

One of the most important and, indeed, attractive characteristics which we shall find in *Who's Afraid of Virginia Woolf?* is the dazzling array of devices which Albee utilizes to attract the attention of the characters and audience, engage them deeply in a confrontation with unpleasant realities, and then move them to a purgative **climax**. Although these techniques are seen throughout his plays, they are present here in an orderly progression of increasing intensity. They are: normal verbal exchange, question-answer-contradiction sequences, sharp verbal insult, a running series of arguments punctuated by a variety of physical movements and razor-edged humor, increasing cruelty leading to emotional and/or physical crescendos, game-play (consisting of combinations of these less intense elements and shaped into clearly defined units), pseudo-religious ritual, and death enactment. These devices are blended into a rich and often poetic dramatic movement of conflict and crisis which fully demonstrates Albee's skilled artistry. Each of these elements will be examined in discussing the play.

CHARACTERISTICS OF ALBEE'S LANGUAGE

Despite the voluminous critical attention which has been given to Albee's work, the language of the plays has seldom received more than passing analysis. This is unfortunate because Albee is a veritable magician with words - he knows precisely what the auditory and emotive power of words can accomplish. He capitalizes on both the lyrical quality of long speeches and the pounding rhythm of a rapid exchange of insults. Albee also has an ear for the comic and satiric possibilities of the **cliche** in portraying man and his social relationships. Used to such ends, **cliche** becomes a sustained metaphor which is sometimes used as a central thematic motif. An example of this is the creation of the American Dream boy who is nothing more than a pastiche of clippings and pictures from American bourgeois magazines. Together with **cliche**, Albee combines puns, allusions, onomatopoeia, and repetition to create a rich verbal texture which can, as one critic has said, take on an intrinsic interest of its own which is quite apart from the actual dramatic action.

What is particularly noticeable about the language of the confrontation process, especially in *Who's Afraid of Virginia Woolf?*, is the many types of language which are combined into the dramatic text. Language assumes the function of dialectic in moving the characters and action from the exposition through to the **climax** and final resolution - a movement from illusion to truthful awareness and communication. The variation, juxtaposition, and repetition of moods of language (comic, satiric, insulting, etc.) and types of speech constructions (long moving speeches, question-and-answer sequences, etc.) - succeed in giving the language an extremely high effectiveness which is capable of penetrating the emotional cores of the characters.

An attractive quality of Albee's language is his comic dialogue: it is sometimes sheer slapstick, as in the brief scene between Julian and the "old hag" in *Tiny Alice*; or it can come in catty exchanges of petty insults as those between Mommy and Daddy in *The American Dream* and between Claire and Agnes in *A Delicate Balance*. As we noted in discussing *The American Dream*, such dialogue utilizes all the comic possibilities of cliched expressions and topics of conversation which people can dredge up in order to find something to talk about. If one listens to this dialogue, it becomes apparent that there is little communication value in it. Like Ionesco, Albee succeeds in characterizing the stereotyped and essentially empty social relationships which are found so often in modern society.

In *Who's Afraid of Virginia Woolf?* there are two main types of comic language: that intended for comic relief, as in the discussion of Honey's tendency to vomit at the least emotion; and the **black humor**, the comedy which is both wildly funny yet injected for a serious purpose. This language of **black humor** is used in the running battle of furious insults between Martha and George and only veils the deep bitterness and emotional tension which fills each character. It is the type of language seen often in Beckett and Genet and is designed to carry a "double edge" which enables a balance between sanity and sheer madness. In noting the serious purpose of the comic language and the laughter which it evokes, one is reminded of the dark laughter of Hawthorne's Ethan Brand who, he wrote, "does not laugh like a man that is glad." Thus the wild humor which fills

Albee's battle of the sexes is more of a symptom for the furious madness which is scarcely beneath the surface of emotions, and it certainly does not make the play any less painful to watch, but instead only twists the emotional spring even tighter.

The type of language for which Albee is most noted is that used by the combatants in the running battle of the sexes - Mommy and Daddy, Nurse and Intern, Martha and George. It is a powerful language of ridicule, taunts, scrapes, **black humor**, and mutual recrimination and humiliation. These characters' games of one-upsmanship elicit volleys of insult which sometimes rise in intensity to the point at which they are climaxed by an act of violence - a slap on the face or even a violent attack. Such abrasiveness in the relationship of the sexual partners is intended to dramatize Albee's conception, albeit a severe one, of a social relationship marked by an absence of love and tenderness and one which is quite often self-destructive for the participants. This kind of language in the female is indicative of her drive for dominance over the male and thus the male has no choice but to fight back as best he can, which in the cases of Intern and George, is sometimes so successful that it spurs the female to even greater heights of counterblast. In sum, it succeeds in characterizing the private worlds of the participants as individual hells in which there is no limit to what lengths the characters will go in hurting each other. Such hostility makes a mockery of social relationship and especially of the home, in the case of *Who's Afraid of Virginia Woolf?* - in the words of Shakespeare in *As You Like It*: "This is no place, this house is but a butchery."

The virulence of the language in *The Death of Bessie Smith* conveys the tormented emotional state of the Nurse and Intern and is expressive of their frustrated desire to escape the stagnated world in which they are trapped. The language of the Nurse in her cruelty to the men in the hospital and in her writhing self-revelatory speech at the end of the play are symptomatic of her spiritual sterility. In this play as well as in *Who's Afraid of Virginia Woolf?* the cathartic effect of the action is achieved primarily through the language rather than through physical action or bloody spectacle. The absence of Bessie, for example, increases the importance of what is said in conveying the impact and tragic implications of her violent death. Similarly, the death of the child in the latter play is a symbolic one achieved through verbal ritual. But even in plays which contain the spectacle of a violent death as in *The Zoo Story* and *Tiny Alice*, the powerful eloquence and the thematic importance of the characters' death speeches contribute as much to the catharsis as does the actual act of violence.

The virtuosity of Albee's language is superbly demonstrated in *Who's Afraid of Virginia Woolf?* in which every element is calculated to contribute toward the effect of the play - even Martha's abundant "Hunh's" and the seemingly never-ending string of petty insults. One aspect of the play which shocked audiences when it was first produced in 1962 was the obscene language, all of which is, quite characteristically, delivered by Martha. (Before the play could open in Boston the public censor expunged twelve obscenities from the text and held that fifty-four additional usages were highly questionable.) But what is important is that this language does not violate the economy or the integrity of the work. Such language is purposely abrasive because Albee uses it to construct a closed universe of bitterness and destructive illusion.

MOTIFS IN ALBEE'S PLAYS

One can get some idea of Albee's major concerns by realizing that at least five major motifs recur with varying degrees of emphasis and in varying combinations throughout Albee's thirteen plays. They are: cruelty and violence, sexual strife, homosexuality and sterility.

CRUELTY AND VIOLENCE

One of the major realizations underlying Albee's drama is that cruelty and violence are basic to man's nature. Despite the fact that he lives in a supposedly sophisticated civilization, the archetypal relationship of attacker and victim still remain descriptive of man's behavior in society; perhaps Nietzsche was correct in saying that "Man is the cruelest animal." As we have already noted, Albee expresses cruelty and violence through his language of abuse and explosive screams of insult which are intended to penetrate to the core of a person's emotions. Specifically stated, cruelty and violence fulfill three major functions in Albee's plays:

First, cruelty and violence are part of the outward manifestations of a closed, static world in which normal communications and feeling have withered away and in which the characters are profoundly unhappy. The characters in *The Death of Bessie Smith* and *Who's Afraid of Virginia Woolf?* are driven to mistreat each other so bitterly by a deep, nagging despair at their life situations; theirs is a world of spiritual decay and sterility in which all hope for growth of affection has been negated by an ever-increasing frustration and anger which, ironically, only serves to make that world more inescapable -it is a literal hell on earth. The characters can function in society, i.e., outside the closed circle, only because they maintain vicious "in-fighting" which is an outlet for their frustration. This "hell" is no specific geographical location - it can be a supposedly life-saving hospital or the living room of an upper-middle-class home. In the case of *The Ballad of the Sad Café*, in which the characters are both physically and spiritually sterile, it is a public gathering place - a tormented battle takes place there and when it ends, the café has been made permanently scarred and sterile.

In *A Delicate Balance* and *All Over*, these two motifs are employed to depict first the illusion of the home as a haven from reality, and in the second case, a parental relationship which has become perverted beyond all recognition. But in each case - that of Julia's panic and the hate of mother and daughter - there has ceased to be a growth of spirituality; there is rather a total misuse of the family unit.

Secondly, cruelty and violence can function as an elemental form of communication. In *The Zoo Story*, for example, Jerry must resort to physical violence in order to penetrate Peter's isolation. Albee feels that illusion makes true communications impossible because it surrounds man in his own sterile and impenetrable world. In *Who's Afraid of Virginia Woolf?*, verbal cruelty becomes the only form of communication between George and Martha because it reaches their most elemental sensibilities. All others have become inoperative and numb.

Third, Albee makes use of cruelty and violence to help achieve the task of making his characters face the reality of their lives. Thus it becomes an important part in the confrontation process in *Who's Afraid of Virginia Woolf?* in which the characters are engaged in violent and cruel games intended to propel them to the destruction of their illusions. These motifs thus become both symptom and tool in constructing a play which is intended to lull an audience from its own illusions and complacency.

SEXUAL STRIFE

In every play Albee has written which contains a relationship between male and female, there is some kind of strife between the sexes - Albee has never created a truly healthy heterosexual relationship. As we have noted, the initial introduction of this conflict appeared with Mommy and Daddy in *The American Dream* and has appeared regularly since then - even in *All Over*, it has been suggested that we have the final chapter in the saga of Mommy and Daddy. Although most of the female and male characters are endowed with far greater dimensions than his original couple, the paradigm is consistent and Albee uses it as a vehicle for his examination of the failings of both the individual and society in general.

HOMOSEXUALITY

The motif of homosexuality has been the cause of considerable debate among critics because its function in a play is often in doubt. It appears in three forms: 1) blatant homosexual attraction as in two of Albee's adaptations, *The Ballad of the Sad Café* and *Malcolm*; 2) both explicit and firmly implied references to past and/or present homosexual liaisons and experiences - those of Jerry and the gardener's son, Lawyer and Cardinal, Cardinal and Julian, Julian and Butler; 3) intimations of homosexuality - *The Zoo Story*, for example, has been said to contain a rather elaborate **parody** of a homosexual propositioning and a sexual act, and in *Tiny Alice* it has been suggested that Julian's sexual reveries are far too heavily tinged with homosexual overtones.

It is on these bases that Albee has been accused of having a "homosexual vision," but there is considerable reason to question such an appraisal. First of all, it is true that the two adaptations which are mentioned have exaggerated the presence of homosexuality which was contained in the original works; however, it is important to note that the entire plays themselves are overwritten and rather poorly written. Thus one should not attach major relevance to works for which the author himself has apologized. Second, the many confusing references to male relationships in *Tiny Alice* are not essential to the thematic development of the drama but are there primarily to add to the pervasive air of ambiguity presented. The presence of homosexual suggestions in Jerry's encountering Peter has either been disputed or completely ignored by some critics and stressed by others - it is unclear as to what is there, but it should be noted that Albee has denied that such things exist in his plays. Thus, homosexuality is a prominent motif in Albee's work, but it is never exactly clear how Albee feels about its function as a dramatic device.

STERILITY

The world which Albee's characters inhabit, filled with hostility, cruelty and illusion, continually evokes images of "The Waste Land" - a view of the modern world in which both physical and spiritual sterility is pervasive. Physical sterility is nearly a commonplace condition in Albee's plays: the child of Mommy and Daddy (if it was a real one) and of Tobias and Agnes died in their early years; the relationships of Mommy and Daddy, Nurse and Intern, George and Martha, Miss Amelia and Cousin Lyman, Julia and her four husbands, and the daughter and her husband in *All Over* - are all now childless and void of tenderness and love their physical sterility is a symptom, therefore, of their spiritual sterility. Likewise, the lifeless and life-letting ejaculation of Julian at the end of *Tiny Alice* is perhaps the most emphatic statement of the sterility and waste inherent in illusion. The scenes which Albee presents throughout his plays are predominantly sad ones depicting the lives of waste and torment which his characters lead - a vision which often causes one to overlook the fact that illusions can be destroyed.

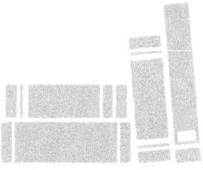

THE ZOO STORY

It is unknown what specific events may have brought about the abrupt end of a decade of writing what Albee has termed "mediocre" verse and the sudden beginning of a brilliant career as playwright; however, in 1958 Albee wrote *The Zoo Story* in three weeks' time. According to Albee's vague account, the writing of the play came at the end of a long period of depression during which he had given up his job as a Western Union messenger. No doubt this confrontation with self crystallized his years of preparation spent in reading, writing, and talking with artists in Greenwich Village coffee houses.

The Zoo Story, a one-act play, was first read by a number of New York producers and rejected. Albee's close friend, William Flanagan, then sent the script to David Diamond, an American composer living in Italy and he, in turn, forwarded it to a Swiss actor, Pinkar Brown. Brown made a tape recording of the play, acting both roles, and sent it to the head of the drama department of a major publishing house in Frankfurt. Finally, the play was accepted and produced by Boleslaw Barlog at the Schiller Theater Werkstatt in Berlin, on September 28, 1959 - on the same bill with Beckett's *Krapp's Last Tape*. After touring twelve German cities and being enthusiastically acclaimed, *The Zoo Story* opened at a Greenwich Village theater, The Provincetown Playhouse, on January 14, 1960.

The Zoo Story (along with *The American Dream*) identifies Albee with the European Theater of the Absurd, an association which still lingers today. This first play is a highly significant work because it contains both a sophisticated degree of artistry and an important statement of Albee's thematic concerns, which have remained consistent throughout the works with varying areas of emphasis. The two major **themes** of the play are: first, the shallowness and meaninglessness of contemporary American society, including its self-righteous values and mores, religious hypocrisy, and self-complacent everyday life; secondly, the corresponding self-isolation of man in this kind of society who has surrounded himself in an illusion of wellbeing and self-satisfaction. The embodiment of these serious shortcomings of man and society is Peter, a middle-aged, impeccably dressed businessman whose life is filled with bland inanities: a lack-luster childless marriage, suburban home, a parakeet, a bookshelf stocked with current best sellers, etc. Peter is not so much an Everyman, as he is a personification of these characteristics. He is, in effect, a very small man who exudes an air of boredom and spiritual vacuity.

Jerry, the **protagonist** of the play, on the other hand, is certainly the more interesting and more complex character. On an obvious level, he is strikingly different in appearance - a once handsome and muscular man whose appearance has become extremely unkept and whose strong build has become fat. Jerry's living habits are irregular and rather uncouth; in sum, he is set in direct contrast with Peter. The dramatic conflict of the play is a confrontation, verbal and physical, in which Jerry takes it upon himself to penetrate the isolation in which Peter lives and to expose and revitalize his long-hidden and dormant humanity. Jerry is to be a savior, a modern-day Orpheus who sacrifices himself for Peter's salvation, which, in Albee's view, is being able and willing to communicate. The dramatic structure of the play is an ordered, ritualistic movement of three parts which can be best described as tracing the progression from a life of illusion and isolation to one of awareness.

The most arresting and even mystifying aspect of the play is Jerry's unrelenting compulsion to accomplish Peter's salvation. He attempts to convey to Peter the story of what happened to him while he was at the zoo that morning - an event of the greatest importance to him and which he feels driven to convey. But given Peter's shallowness and unwillingness to take a sincere interest in another human being, such a simple act of communication is impossible. Thus in order to engage Peter, Jerry mounts a series of attempts which range from a simple question-and-answer sequence to Jerry's climactic suicide-death. It is only through this ultimate sacrifice that Peter is finally reached.

Among the most significant elements of the play is the long parable Jerry delivers about his encounter with an ugly, nasty black dog, which his ugly, nasty landlady kept at the door of the rooming house. "The Story of Jerry and His Dog" is the account of the way in which he won the dog's acceptance, i.e., the way in which he communicated with the beast and brought him to some kind of understanding. There is an obvious Miltonic **allusion** here to the **episode** in *Paradise Lost* at the gate of Hell through which Satan has to pass on his journey to Eden. The significance of this parable is twofold. First, it functions as a hypnotic, if initially incomprehensible, force on both Peter and the audience, to draw them into a participation or close communion with Jerry who is trying to communicate some deep truth. Second, the story of the encounter is an exact description of the way in which Jerry is attempting to reach Peter. Artistically, the speech is a very beautiful and euphonious passage which reveals at this early date Albee's great capability with language.

The identification of Jerry as a Christ-figure is another intriguing element of the play. Both the parable and his long death speech are rich in Biblical **allusion** and a rising formality of expression which conveys a sense of great seriousness and purpose in what Jerry is attempting. He is, in fact, on a mission to save Peter and has committed himself totally to that task. The Biblical quality of the language, the religious symbols, and the final cathartic event, which is suggestive of a bloody Crucifixion enactment, create a sense of religious ritual, a device which appears in both *Who's Afraid of Virginia Woolf?* and *Tiny Alice*.

Jerry's final sacrifice affects a drastic change in Peter's life - he is now able to recognize the truth about the state of his life and the immensity of what he has just witnessed. These realizations come in an instant moment of shocking recognition which is one of the more effective scenes in Albee's theater. But even though Peter's salvation is a highly dramatic event, our sustained attention is on Jerry because he is not only a Christ-figure who has fulfilled a great mission, but he is also a kind of existential hero who has freely chosen to encounter Peter on a uniquely individual basis and to do whatever necessary to end his isolation. The salvation is a purely personal one in which one man has tried simply to communicate with another. There is no indication in the characterization of Jerry that Albee considered him a maniac or a homosexual fanatic (as some critics have asserted) - he is totally lucid.

Albee's main points of emphasis seem to be that, first of all, salvation for a man like Peter is possible, even though it may come at a high price; and secondly, a mere man can freely elect to penetrate the isolation and illusion of another through a direct confrontation. Thus Jerry's sacrifice is a supreme act of love and it is in this that many critics have found a strong affirmation in a play which could easily have concluded in a demonstration of the absurdity of existence.

THE SANDBOX

The Sandbox is a brief one-act play consisting of seven rapidly moving scenes and employing a free usage of lighting effects which range from bright day to total darkness; the performing time is about fourteen minutes. There are four main characters and a musician who plays through the performance. The characters are Mommy and Daddy, a middle-aged couple; Grandma, a very old lady who is about to die; and a Young Man who is later identified as the Angel of Death. *The Sandbox* is nearly identical to a longer one-act play, *The American Dream*, and in **theme** and technique both plays are closely associated with the Theater of the Absurd. The play was written to be performed at the Spoletto Festival of Two Worlds, in Italy. At the time of the commission Albee was in the process of writing *The American Dream* and he accomplished this new task by extracting the major characters from the longer play and placing them in an expressionistic setting - a sandbox, for example, is intended to represent a beach. Actually the play was never performed at the festival, but instead opened in New York at the Jazz Gallery on April 15, 1960.

There is a close thematic continuity between *The Zoo Story* and *The Sandbox* and, of course, *The American Dream*. In *The Sandbox* Albee again attacks the hypocritical sentiments and stereotyped attitudes which were embodied in Peter. In *The*

Sandbox the major emphasis is placed specifically on the social institution of the American family. The family is seen here as a trite relationship which is devoid of sincere affection and true communication. For Albee, the family unit is part of the great American myth, now a meaningless thing, but which in our pioneer days played a hardy and integral role in the development of the nation - America has long since failed to live up to its tradition. In the modern world the typical family is caught up in a mesmerizing commercially-oriented society which has turned the so-called "American Heritage" into a grand illusion and the family, as the most intimate part of this illusion, is a prime example of the absurdity of life in the modern world. But this **theme** is hardly original with Albee-a stereotyped and vacuous family life is one of the basic **themes** of the European Absurdist playwrights, perhaps best dramatized in Ionesco's *The Bald Soprano*. Mommy and Daddy, in *The Sandbox* as well as in *The American Dream*, are representatives of what has been called the phenomenon of Momism - the relationship in the family unit in which the mother is dominant over the male and everyone else in the household; she guards her position of authority with great jealousy and has become, in most respects, the "male " figure of the family. This relationship, which is seen in Strindberg's plays, will be discussed in detail in our analysis of *Who's Afraid of Virginia Woolf?*

The Sandbox also attacks the cliched "American way of death" - replete with its false expressions of sympathy and loss, tender euphemisms, and gawdy display. In fact, the children's true feelings in the play, and often in reality, are the very opposite of bereavement at the death of a parent. The appealing old grandmother in this play, lying in the sandbox waiting to die, humorously mimics Mommy and Daddy's superficial and insincere expressions of concern and sadness. They are, in fact, eagerly awaiting the "blessed" event of her death and their thinly veiled sentiments might well be described as murderous. Perhaps it is because Albee wrote the play shortly after the death of his own grandmother, to whom he had been closely attached, that the character of Grandma alone is portrayed with any true vitality and honest wit. She is directly contrasted with the dull and disgustingly phony Mommy and Daddy. When Grandma finally dies (the sandbox becomes a coffin), she leaves with a smile and a few tender words, which are the only sincere ones in a play filled with cliches.

A heightened sense of the Absurd is generated by the presence, unexplained and seemingly taken for granted, of two very conspicuous characters - a young, extremely good-looking man in a swimming suit who performs calisthenics throughout the play and then assumes the role of the Angel of Death. The other character is a musician who plays a bass violin during the action. The Young Man, as it turns out, is an aspiring actor who has been sent there, by some unknown person, to play this eerie part, which he does with comic awkwardness, but without any unpleasantness - the final scene in which he gives Grandma the kiss of death, which brings a mischievous grin to her face, is one of touching tenderness.

The obvious theatrical nature of what takes place in the play is meant to convey a sense of the Absurd and to demonstrate in an exaggerated, but truthful sense, the phoniness and sterility in so many of modern man's responses to the realities of life. The close integration of form and content in the play creates a "moving picture" of one aspect of that Absurdity.

FAM AND YAM

Fam and Yam is Albee's least known play and certainly the least appreciated. It is significant more for its expression of the playwright's attitude toward his profession and toward the American Theater Establishment than for its intrinsic literary value. The play was first performed on August 27, 1960 at The White Barn in Westport, Connecticut. Later it appeared with Samuel Beckett's *Embers* and Harry Tierney's *Nekros* as a production of the Greater New York Chapter of ANTA's Matinee Theater Series on February 18, 1963. The play consists simply of a fourteen-page comic satirical interview of an aging Famous American Playwright (called FAM) by a Young American Playwright (YAM). The Young man has requested an interview with this famous figure for the purpose of writing an article assessing the state of the American theater, which has long been a favorite topic with Albee. But in actuality, the interview turns into a penetrating survey of the "Establishment" and at the same time expresses some of the frustration and impatience of young artists attempting to break into a closed system. Thus the play can be considered a formal statement read into the permanent record, so to speak, of Albee's drive for an open, honest theater in which there is room for youthful expression and innovation.

As might be expected, the older playwright, FAM, comes off rather poorly in the interview. His apartment furnishings reflect his formidable success-he owns a plum-colored sofa, two Modigliani's, a Braque, a Motherwell and a Kline; he has attained great success through his art and has surrounded himself with the fine things of life, but in the process has separated himself from the pulsebeat of the theater: the new voices and techniques. During the interview FAM constantly sips brandy and becomes progressively intoxicated. Initially his responses to YAM's questions are trite and non-committal, but under the influence of alcohol, he begins to readily agree with YAM's biting judgments of American producers, directors, critics ("sociological arbiters"), the institution of the "theater party", and actors' unions. By the time the play ends, it becomes apparent that FAM has not heard of anything so absurdly humorous for a long time - the state of the theater with its demigods and financial plotters appears quite antithetical to the true nature of art.

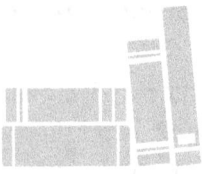

THE DEATH OF BESSIE SMITH

Albee's second major play, *The Death of Bessie Smith*, is a marked departure in technique from *The Zoo Story*, although its **theme** is closely related. In this work Albee has woven into the fabric of a powerful one-act play the story of the tragic death of blues singer Bessie Smith. The potential pathos of her death is self-evident: On September 26, 1937 she was severely injured in a car accident and was then refused medical treatment because of her color, at the all-white Mercy Hospital in Memphis, Tennessee. The play is significant in charting Albee's development as a playwright because, first of all, it combines a public, socially salient **theme** with the private, psychological dimensions of characters created by the dramatist - thus there is an orchestration of the public and private views of a single event. Secondly, the psychological study of the main characters in the hospital foreshadows that of *Who's Afraid of Virginia Woolf?* The play was premiered on April 21, 1960 at the Schlosspark Theater in Berlin and opened at the York Playhouse in New York on March 1, 1961.

The Death of Bessie Smith is Albee's only effort thus far in adapting a specific topical event to drama. No doubt he recognized the possibilities of using such an infamous event of injustice and cruelty to express in another light the spiritual sickness he finds, not only in the South, but throughout society. In terms of Albee's social consciousness there is a continuity running throughout those plays in that they deal with spiritual decay and gross insensitivity and the corresponding need for a revival of communication and love. While the specific **theme** of the play is social injustice and racism, the boundaries of the play are transcended and Albee makes a statement of universal applicability.

The play has been criticized for its structural looseness, especially when one compares it with the near-classical economy of *The Zoo Story* and *The Sandbox*. In the eight scenes of the play there is no cohesive internal development and unification between the external reality of Bessie's accident and the psychological insights we receive into the characters in the hospital. Rather, the two worlds are juxtaposed until the final scene and therefore, each is allowed to contribute its own intrinsic value to the over-all effect of the play. The so-called "public" sphere is represented only by Bessie's husband, Jack, who appears in four of the eight scenes. Bessie herself is a presence rather than an actual character and it has been suggested that Albee avoids a good deal of melodrama by only informing the audience of what has happened to her.

The second scene of the play introduces and quickly characterizes the "private" sphere in which the main figure is the Nurse. The audience's initial introduction to Nurse, in the scene with her father, reveals the climate of the South and of the private sphere as one of bitter racism and the frustration inherent in illusions of would-be importance and success. It is a world in which the inhabitants feel they have been cheated of their true station in life, of the myth of the South - all of which is comparable to the scene of William's *A Streetcar Named Desire*. Nurse takes all of these bitter frustrations and hostility with her to the hospital, the setting of the third scene. Here she is able to wreak some small vengeance on the world by asserting her domineering personality through her position of small authority. Instead of caring for patients, as one would expect her to do, she only sits at the admissions desk from which she both controls entrance into the hospital (specially Bessie's) and abuses the other characters - Orderly, Intern and Second Nurse (they are given only functional names). In temperament, Nurse closely resembles Mommy in *The Sandbox* and *The American Dream* and, as we shall discover, Martha in *Who's Afraid of Virginia Woolf?* She is extremely aggressive, demonstrates a masculine demeanor, has a sharp tongue and is totally intolerant of rebuttal or any indication of encroachment on her authority. She seeks to dominate and manipulate the male world which is somewhat weakly represented by the white Intern who is hopelessly in love with her, and by the light-skinned black Orderly who is willing to endure her taunts in the hope of advancing in white society.

In his characterizations, Albee is somewhat too obvious in revealing where his sentiments rest - all the white characters have functional names, including the would-be white Orderly; they are obviously distorted and even abnormal; and there is repeated reference to the mayor of the town who is recuperating from a hemorrhoid operation. Nevertheless, the message Albee intends rings clear: Bessie Smith's death was not strictly the result of blatant racism, but of a much deeper sickness lying at the heart of society. The Nurse, in Albee's mind, embodies the perversity and pitiable sickness of such an existence. The private world of the hospital is placed in direct contrast with the external world of reality and human exigency: the world of Bessie and Jack begins in exuberance and ends in tragedy; in the hospital, however, there is no such movement. Rather, Albee depicts a static world of stagnant morality and sensibility. The overriding impression in the hospital scenes is one of a virulent, stifled fury which infects all of the characters and eventually reaches outside to kill Bessie. The manifestations of this fury are many: the Nurse's savage humiliation of both the Intern and the contemptible Orderly; the anxious, sexcraved Intern who professes liberal ideas and desires to do something of value in service to humanity, but his lust for Nurse, and probably an even deeper weakness in character, stymies these ambitions. The sexual frustration of Nurse is also an important element to the fury of this private world. Neither she nor Intern seem capable of obtaining sexual satisfaction or, indeed, any kind of satisfaction. Their existences center around a daytime of begrudging service in the hospital, and a night time of sex-play which always stops short of consummation.

In addition to the sexual frustration, another component to the corrosive atmosphere of the hospital is, of course, racial bigotry, which appears in Albee's vision to be a kind of wild madness - Nurse literally screams when Bessie arrives outside the hospital. The irrationality of this hate, however, is only one part of the sickness which pervades the hospital along with frustrated ambitions and sexual desire - these are symptoms of a deep spiritual sterility which manifests itself through their overwhelming cruelty toward Bessie and toward each other. The meeting of the spheres in the final scene only demonstrates the terrible destructiveness which such decay can cause, but this **climax** also elicits Nurse's long speech in which she summarizes the sterility of her life and the world around her - a kind of existential nausea at her state of existence. The play ends in total exhaustion and the Intern alone seems to have changed for the better, since in the moment of crisis, he finally broached Nurse's power over him and thus the possibility is raised that he can eventually escape the stagnant hospital and the South. The affirmation which appeared in *The Zoo Story*, *The Sandbox* and in later plays, is at its weakest in this play.

The language of *The Death of Bessie Smith* has been described as possessing a "euphonic quality which approaches stylization." The use of southern accents by the characters, which some critics consider phony, is quite unobtrusive because our attention is always drawn to the power of the language. It is a rich, emotionally charged language which has the crucial function of characterizing the entire scene of the play - in addition of the dark fury of much of the language in the torrents of insult and abuse, there are also instances of bitter-sweet **satire**, and dialogue which assumes the majestic rhythm of southern speech which approaches verbal melody. One critic has also discovered a finer point of artistry in the language - the repeated play on the word "going," in the sense of "going to do something." All of the characters have ambitions and desires which end in frustration; thus the use of the verb and its ironic conclusion reinforces the stasis of the entire scene.

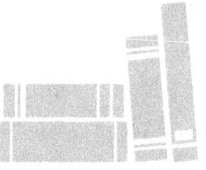

THE AMERICAN DREAM

The American Dream opened at the York Playhouse in New York on January 24, 1961 together with a one-act operatic adaptation, Bartleby, an effort on which William Flanagan, Albee, and several other writers had collaborated. The adaptation was what one critic termed an "admirable failure" and was replaced on the bill by *The Death of Bessie Smith*.

Although *The American Dream*, a long one-act play, elicited strongly favorable critical response, it is in some respects a less perfect play than either *The Zoo Story* or its off-shoot, *The Sandbox*. Most noticeably, it lacks the economy and close integration of form and content which made both former plays exciting examples of the dramatic clarity and precision which Albee is capable of producing. It is also a far less original play than the others, purposely taking its more obvious technical effects and artifices from the Absurdist farces, especially Ionesco's *The Bald Soprano*. The play is very significant, however, because it is a major effort by an American playwright to introduce the techniques of the Theater of the Absurd to American audiences. In addition to *Who's Afraid of Virginia Woolf?*, this is probably Albee's best known play and has consistently identified him with the Absurdist movement.

Albee moved the setting of *The American Dream* indoors from an expressionistic beach scene to a realistic living-room setting furnished with all the conventional "comforts" of the middle-class American family living room. The Trio of major characters are identical with those of *The Sandbox* - Mommy, Daddy and Grandma. The same tension exists here between Mommy and Grandma as they continually trade sharp insults and Mommy again makes it clear that she wishes to dispose of the old woman, who has supposedly become a nuisance. This play contains much more **satire** and fewer moments of tenderness than *The Sandbox* and Grandma is in especially good form: throughout the play she demonstrates a beautifully acerbic wit and scheming imagination that seems quite incongruous with a person of her great age. But through this winning manner, she can also be quite as cruel as her daughter - for example, she seeks to hurt her daughter by revealing to the visitor, Mrs. Barker, the tragic story (filled with Absurdist overtones) of Mommy and Daddy's "unsatisfactory child" which had died years before. As in *Who's Afraid of Virginia Woolf?*, the child who never appears is a spectre which haunts the parents and accounts for some of their present bitterness and tremendous cynicism, as well as making them vulnerable to cruel attack. The running conflict between Mommy and Grandma continues until the eighth scene when Grandma takes the initiative and plots with the Young Man who by chance "happens" to knock on their apartment door (reminiscent of the fireman in *The Bald Soprano*).

In addition to bitterly satirizing the absence of feeling and downright hostility between husband and wife, parent and child, and the American proclivity toward disposing of old people by sending them off to rest homes, Albee also echoes Ionesco in satirizing the meaningless platitudes of conversation and social **convention** - first in the opening dialogue between Mommy and Daddy about a beige hat which Mommy has purchased, and later upon the arrival of Mrs. Barker, the president of Mommy's ladies club, who is promptly invited to come in and take off her dress. Another object of Albee's focus is the bitterly sterile marital relationship between Mommy and Daddy. Mommy is clearly the masculine force in the family and she dominates both her husband and the entire household. The sexual sterility of their marriage is explicitly revealed as Mommy boasts that only she could obtain sexual satisfaction and that Daddy should be happy that she ever allowed him to approach her.

In sum, there is only minimal plot development in the play; rather, it is primarily an examination and biting **satire** of the American family unit. The inanities of everyday family life, the hypocrisy of sentiment, the total lack of meaningful communication and the dominance of the female over the weak, dutiful male - are all targets of Albee's indictment and work together to create an extremely humorous and entertaining play. It is quite as delightful and every bit as effective as Ionesco's *The Bald Soprano*, but it has, however, been adapted to an extremely recognizable American idiom.

The two minor characters of *The American Dream*, Mrs. Barker and the Young Man, are purely functional; their presence contributes to the Absurdist quality of the play and they become instruments in both Grandma's drive to hurt her daughter and in her final coup. Mrs. Barker, like Ionesco's fireman and the Young Man in this play, has no idea why she has arrived at this particular apartment, but she comes and sits quietly in a slip throughout the play, acting as a bouncing board for Grandma's biting quips and cruel revelations. The Young Man, tall, lean and handsome, is the embodiment of the American Dream. Added to this ostensibly perfect physical perfection is his great sex appeal, which is demonstrated by both Mommy and Grandma's attraction to him, placing them further at odds; moreover, he is a midwesterner, a middle-American lad who was raised into healthy manhood on a farm and, like most Americans in Albee's view, is willing to do anything for money. Obviously Albee intends this creature to be a personification of what he sees as the most admired traits in American society, the middle-class hero figure possessing movie-magazine virtues. Yet Albee reveals a major flaw in this creation - the Young Man is not able to obtain any real satisfaction - sexual or emotional; he is, in effect, an empty shell whose body is to be used by others. *The American Dream*, then, is a sad creature who represents a strong indictment of what Albee sees in American society - false values, spiritual shallowness behind an attractive, stereotyped edifice.

The play abounds in devices and motifs found in the Absurdist Theater of Ionesco: cliches' and puns; the dialogue of inanities demonstrating the vacuity of language and inability to communicate; the proliferation of objects seen in Grandma's strange, neatly wrapped boxes; the abrupt and incongruous action, as in Mrs. Barker's disrobing; the disappearance of objects - Grandma's television, her bedroom, and the kitchen; and, of course, the unexpected arrival of guests. Thus the effect of the play is achieved through a combination of comic and sometimes pathetic absurdity, which forms an unrelenting **satire** of American values and social conventions.

Despite the fact that *The American Dream* was written with the intention of utilizing Absurdist techniques and that it is a harsh attack on our society, it remains thematically consistent with the rest of Albee's work. In this play and in *The Sandbox* there is an unmistakable **refrain** of affirmation and an unconquered life-spirit represented by the vibrant Grandma who in this play is shown to survive in time to laugh at the ridiculousness of her miserably petty children. Although she is dead to the other characters, she stands outside the drama at the end of the play and watches the group celebrate the arrival of the Young Man whose perfection is infinitely more acceptable to her daughter than her own great age. She becomes the narrator of the celebration and like Puck, can point out "what fools these mortals be."

In an interview in 1965, Albee confirmed such an interpretation by saying that Grandma does not really die in the play, except in the eyes of the other characters. Rather, she continues to exist on another plane of being. Thus there seems to a possibility of hope left in the world in that the spirit represented in Grandma has not died, but that it might well appear again in better times.

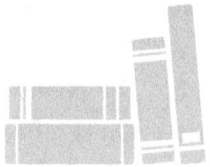

WHO'S AFRAID OF VIRGINIA WOOLF?

INTRODUCTION

The work for which Albee is best known, *Who's Afraid of Virginia Woolf?*, opened on Broadway on October 13, 1962 at the Billy Rose Theater. Its fine cast included Uta Hagen as Martha, Arthur Hill as George, George Grizzard as Nick, and Melinda Dillon as Honey. The show ran on Broadway for two years and, for a much longer time, appeared throughout the nation and around the world. It received both the New York Drama, Critics' and Tony Awards for the best play of the 1962-63 season, and it also won an award given by the Association of the Foreign Press. *Who's Afraid of Virginia Woolf?* has appeared in most major European cities and in countries throughout the world including South Africa, Japan, Mexico, Chile, Israel, Uruguay, Argentina, Czechoslovakia, and Poland. In Prague the play appeared as *Who's Afraid of Franz Kafka?*, largely because the audience was not familiar with the nursery **rhyme** which inspired the rather strange title which Albee gave his play. One critic also noted that the Czech producers wanted to convey a strong sense of the "bureaucratic nightmare of the external world ... and the feeling of unreasoning inexpiable guilt which compresses the individual."

Together with its long run on Broadway and productions throughout the world, the play is said to have made Albee one of the most often performed American playwrights. Despite the major awards the play had already received, the Pulitzer Prize was denied it; John Mason Brown and John Gassner, who had enthusiastically recommended the play, resigned in protest against the selection committee's negative decision. In 1966 the film version of the play was produced, starring Elizabeth Taylor and Richard Burton, and directed by Mike Nichols. Fortunately, only one scene, at the roadhouse, was added to Albee's stage text. This, however, was extraneous and only served to distort the focus of the play from the very private atmosphere of George and Martha's living room.

There are several obvious continuities between this play and what Albee had written earlier. The play is particularly similar in emotional intensity and naturalistic setting with that of *The Death of Bessie Smith*. Also, *Who's Afraid of Virginia Woolf?* is a central link in Albee's penetrating study of the American family unit and of the relationship between husband and wife in modern society. In dealing with such concerns Albee is demonstrating a very strong social commitment which has remained the basis of all his drama. Around the often caricaturized figures of Mommy and Daddy, which are so often seen in television situation-comedy shows, Albee has constructed a very powerful and challenging body of works. We shall examine *Who's Afraid of Virginia Woolf?* in considerable detail in a later chapter.

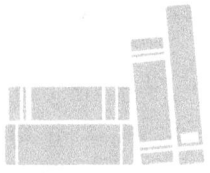

THE BALLAD OF THE SAD CAFÉ

Albee has attempted three adaptations, all of which were unfavorably received because they were markedly inferior to his original works. Restrictions of plot and characterization which are necessarily involved in adapting the work of another author to the stage, in each case, seem to have robbed Albee of his sharp wit and gift of dazzling dialogue. Rather, what has resulted is an amorphous, awkward play which fails to take on an internal, unified life of its own.

Albee's first adaptation, and probably his most successful one, is based on Carson McCullers' Southern Gothic novella, *The Ballad of the Sad Café*. The production came as a disappointing anticlimax to *Who's Afraid of Virginia Woolf?* and was said by critics to be remindful of Albee's fallibility. The play opened on Broadway on October 30, 1963 and featured Colleen Dewhurst as Miss Amelia and Michael Dunn as Cousin Lymon. The setting of the play is the café of Miss Amelia Evans near the town of Society City, Georgia. The time is August, the heat is oppressive, close. Miss McCullers' story, adapted by Albee in unusually faithful detail, centers around a love trio: Miss Amelia is a six foot-two inch giantess, frigid, sexually dwarfed; her mother had died in childbirth, which has had an impact on Amelia who has assumed a masculine manner in attempting to suppress her femininity. Another member of the triangle is Cousin Lymon

Willis, a distant relative of Amelia. He is a dwarfed hunchback, effeminate, a homosexual with a shy, coy personality which is described in the play as that of a young girl. Finally, there is Marvin Macyp, a rough, masculine figure who once married Amelia and was deeply in love with her. She refused to allow their marriage to be consummated, however, and he left in anger. He returns seeking revenge on her, not to conquer her body but to subdue her callous spirit. The love triangle goes through a crisis which functions similarly to that in *Who's Afraid of Virginia Woolf?*, but it is seriously lacking in specific focus. Nevertheless, what emerges after the battle is a clear characterization of the sentiments and motivations which are at play among the members.

Two factors which make the play unwieldy and weak in intensity are the presence of a large cast of townspeople and a narrator-stage manager. The original purpose of the large cast in Miss McCullers' story was that it should function as a chorus in commenting on the various events of the play, for example, the arrival of the strange little man, Cousin Lymon. In the adaptation, however, they become cumbersome spectators who fill the air with their phony and unintentionally comic Southern dialect. Albee has also been criticized for his use of Southern dialect in *The Death of Bessie Smith*, but here artificiality is much more annoying since there are so many more characters.

A second major detriment to the over-all quality of the play is the use of a narrator-stage manager, quite similar to the same figure in Thornton Wilder's *Our Town*. Unlike Wilder's narrator, however, this man does not join in the drama, nor does he have any connection with the town, its people, or the central dramatic action. In fact, one major criticism of the play has been that he has no reason or motivation whatever for telling the story. He delivers long speeches about the nature of love and comments about the characters - all of which are taken verbatim from Miss McCullers' book. Critics have called this inordinate usage an artistic "cop-out" on Albee's part, since he seems to have given material to the narrator which he found difficult to translate into dramatic idiom. To further diminish the effectiveness of the narrator was the use of a black actor in the Broadway production. This was taken as a silent racial implication, which was quite unintended.

As the narrator informs us at the beginning, the play relates two stories - about how Miss Amelia came to open a café which quickly became a popular gathering place for the townspeople, and how the café was destroyed and Miss Amelia became a recluse. The tale is a grotesque love story in which the most violent and destructive powers of love are brought into play. It is also about the uses to which people can put love and about the thin line which separates hate and love. The pivotal character, Miss Amelia, has a deep aggressive need to give of her love, but an accompanying fear and revulsion at being loved. She is a woman somewhat like Martha who cannot find satisfaction in a normal love relationship because she is not able to give totally of herself - whatever is given must be on her terms and thus she jealously guards her dominant position. Both women are possessed by haunting fears and sterile spirits which poison their personality. Miss Amelia cruelly spurns the sexual love of her husband after greedily accepting his gifts and leading him on to expect a normal union. The true nature of Miss Amelia's abnormality is demonstrated when she finally finds someone on whom she can heap her affection without being pressured to accept sexual contact or even genuine emotional involvement. Cousin Lymon, the homosexual dwarf, proves to be totally compatible with her emotional needs - in fact, he thrives on the attention and affection she bestows on him while he offers nothing whatsoever in return, but only makes incessant material demands on her. It is under his influence that she opens the café and becomes an extroverted, generally pleasant person; this strange, perverted love relationship brings Miss Amelia into so-called "bloom." But both Miss McCullers and Albee make it clear that such a saprophytic relationship can have no future and is ultimately destructive. This is soon demonstrated as Cousin Lymon falls in love with Marvin Macy and a three-way love struggle ensues in which each participant attempts to use the other in the interest of his own selfish motives. As Miss Amelia battles Marvin for possession of Lymon, the disgusting hunchback pits the two against each other and sits back delightedly enjoying the spectacle.

Cousin Lymon, it is made apparent, is a Machiavellian grotesque who is meant to be the embodiment of all the evil, perverse and destructive aspects of love. The quality of love is, after all, dependent upon those persons who create that love; this creature thrives upon and in turn feeds the sick emotional needs of Miss Amelia and ultimately is the main force which turns her into a recluse. Such an examination of perverse and destructive love would understandably appeal to Albee since he has repeatedly examined the maladjusted love relationships of people who are close together yet very far apart and who use the relationship to their own ends.

In addition to the structural awkwardness of Albee's adaptation, the play has been criticized as presenting a far too perverted and grotesque picture, which obliterates any meaningful message. This becomes apparent when one compares the ending of *The Ballad of the Sad Café* with, for example, that of *Who's Afraid of Virginia Woolf?* In the latter play there is certainly a great amount of abnormality and bitter emotion, but this is finally ameliorated by the climactic purgative movement of the last act - the audience is able to experience a cathartic release. In this play, however, no such relief is offered as Miss Amelia is left to a life of bitter solitude and her café is viciously destroyed - the final scene is one of total despair and sterility. In sum, the inadequacy of the artistry and the forlorn conclusion make *The Ballad of the Sad Café* a depressing shadow on a brilliant career.

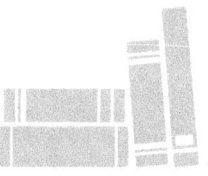

TINY ALICE

Two years after *Who's Afraid of Virginia Woolf?* Albee again aroused a great deal of controversy with *Tiny Alice*. The play has been variously called an allegory, a farce, a homosexual dream play, and Absurdist melodrama, and a statement of Albee's apocalyptic vision. Its effect on critics and audiences has been a mixture of confusion and, strangely enough, anger. One reviewer reacted to the play's complexity by writing, "I am not even certain I can describe adequately enough of the surface plot to provide some idea of what takes place." And another writer said, "In Tallulah Bankhead's famous phrase, there may be less to this than meets the eye." *Tiny Alice* is certainly Albee's most enigmatic play and one of his most innovative. Although many people find the play far too abstruse, few can deny that it is rich in meaning and that it generates a powerful dramatic effect. *Tiny Alice* opened at the Billy Rose Theater on December 29, 1964 with a superb cast directed by Alan Schneider - Sir John Gielgud in the role of Julian and Irene Worth as Miss Alice.

In the most general terms, the play concerns the seduction of a religious brother, Julian, by an apparently omnipotent, but vaguely defined deific force called Tiny Alice, who dwells in a gigantic, perfectly detailed model castle. Despite an intricate maze of plot detail and involved and confusing symbolic elements, the major **theme** is man's need for and dependence on the Ineffable in facing the reality of existence. Albee is concerned with the false sense of security which man derives from his Deity and satirizes the arbitrary manner in which he defines its power and nature. *Tiny Alice* is a morality play in the medieval tradition replete with stage comedy and violence and an enactment of an erotic death scene in which the Christ-figure is pathetically attacked and dragged across the stage in a bloody spectacle. It thus seeks to affect a religious experience in the audience in order that its statement about the state of man's existence will have an optimum effectiveness.

The enigmatic abstract force called Tiny Alice is not a specifically Christian deity, but is intended to embody those elements which seem to appeal, in Albee's view, to the primitive nature of man. Hence, "she" or "it" is not only omnipotent, but also greedy for the total possession of man in the spiritual as well as physical sense. The traditional characteristics of a religious conversion are radically altered to appeal to both Julian's spiritual and sexual needs; in the final scene of the play the close relationship between religious and sexual ecstasy is dramatically posited. Another relationship which Albee probes is that of faith and sanity. Julian is a modern-day spiritual Everyman - he is weak, easily confused, afraid of reality and overwhelmed by the "sublime", and has a burning desire to "serve", to be of some appreciable use. He seeks, in effect, some **metaphysical** focus to which he can swear allegiance and acknowledge his inferiority, and on which he can lay all his doubts and fears in exchange for blind, unquestioning faith. Thus Albee is attempting to portray the religious state of man as being one in which religion serves as an illusion, an "opiate for the masses" which shields its participants from reality. Julian is entirely human, pathetic and lovable in turn, a dupe and martyr at the end.

The pretext for Julian's willing "seduction" is that he is sent on a mission for the Catholic Church, but it is in actuality an elaborately contrived scheme to bring him into contact with Tiny Alice and is masterminded and carried out by her agents. They are: Miss Alice, who describes herself as a surrogate and priestess of Tiny Alice, is middle-aged, very attractive and has the task of becoming deeply involved with Julian, winning his love and then turning him over to Tiny Alice. The other members of this team have only functional names - Lawyer is the most disagreeable of the characters, possessing a fiery, demonic character, which gives us some idea of the nature of the deity he represents. He seems to enjoy his job, not only in directing the conversion-seduction of Julian but also in keeping Miss Alice in line when she begins to show some sincere affection for Julian as he is unwittingly lured into submission. Finally, Butler is the most humorous of the characters and is little more than automation who mouths his lines, giving the clear impression that he is acting a role which has been assigned to him. Furthermore, he appears to be a homosexual who has had a relationship with Lawyer in the past and who seems to develop a strong affection for Julian. The final character in the play is Cardinal, Julian's immediate superior; he is a weak man who engages in a most unpriestly exchange of mocking insults with the Lawyer, a former schoolmate. His obvious greed in the name of the Church's welfare, and his easy acquiescence to Julian's doomed fate, make him a despicable figure and a satirical reflection on the organized Church.

There are many elements in the play which generate the ambiguity and religious mystery which has proved so confusing to audiences. The most noticeable of these is the model castle, placed conspicuously on stage-right. During the course of the play we are made aware that it is the earthly dwelling place of Tiny Alice and is thus somehow eerily involved in the strange events which takes place in the large castle, the home of Miss Alice. What does the model represent and who is Tiny Alice? One of the most curious aspects of the model, first of all, is that there is a model in the living room of the model, and presumably, a model within that, ad infinitum. The most probable interpretation of this vortex structure is that it ultimately becomes nothing - what seems to be a **metaphysical** core to which Julian can give ultimate service is ultimately his own desire to give service, his personally created god which serves an extremely personal and sacred purpose. Thus the model and the spirit of Tiny Alice is the key element in Julian's inability to differentiate between illusion and reality, symbol and substance. As all attention is drawn toward the model and as Julian is finally confronted with leaving this world and joining that of Tiny Alice, it becomes necessary to define what Julian is actually offering himself to. The haunting spectre arises that he has misdirected his faith and now his life to committing himself to an illusion, an attractive shadow on the wall of Plato's cave; what he has thought to be the opportunity for ultimate fulfillment turns out to be only the illusion of that fulfillment.

In addition to the imposing problem of the model, the play literally explodes with all kinds of symbols and vague intimations - Biblical allusions in Julian's death speech, his obvious identification as a Christ-figure, the fire in the chapel, the bounding heart beat which fills the theater, the erotic communion of Julian and Miss Alice in which he is infolded in her arms, etc. It is a kind of surreal mixture of verbal and mimetic **allusions** which, when one attempts to fit them into an understandable picture, remain veiled in confusion and mystery. One strong implication of these confusing signs and symbols is that Albee is demonstrating how easily one can become totally involved in the outward accouterments of religion without ever having to really define his beliefs and the real purpose of his commitment. Religion, in essence, can become a shallow illusion with no real core of solid, substantive meaning - symbol is all! The spirit of Tiny Alice, then, is an elaborate theatrical, and ultimately tragic hoax demonstrating man's ready willingness and even profound need to create an anthropomorphic crutch, a deity cast in his own image, which is used to shield him from reality.

Thus *Tiny Alice* is indeed a surreal dream play as well as a mystery play which dramatizes man's search for and his reliance on the Ineffable as a source of comfort in the face of reality and is therefore closely related to the **theme** of *Who's Afraid of Virginia Woolf?* Julian's final orgiastic union with his bride, Tiny Alice, demonstrates the destructiveness inherent in succumbing to the attraction of illusion. The elaborate seduction process which we witness is merely the enactment in exaggerated terms of yielding to man's natural insecurity. Albee has summed up the meaning of his play quite concisely: "It's a mystery play, a double mystery, and also a morality play, about truth and illusion, the substitute images we create ... easy virtues easy Gods, all the Gods that we create in our own image."

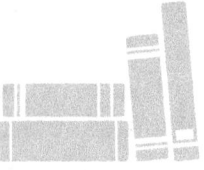

MALCOLM

Two years after *Tiny Alice* was produced, Albee introduced his second adaptation, this one based on James Purdy's novel *Malcolm*. The play opened at the Schubert Theater on January 11, 1966 and closed after seven performances. It is unanimously agreed that *Malcolm* is by far Albee's worst play - even Mr. Albee felt compelled publicly to acknowledge the unfavorable response and apologized two days after the opening. Critical consensus was quite simply that the play was both poorly written and poorly directed; some critics, however, became extremely vehement and called the play a sordid collection of "refuse." While the play has done little, if any, serious damage to Albee's reputation, it once more demonstrated that the adaptation is not his forte. Two matters, however, should concern us at least briefly: first, the main reasons for the play's failure; and second, it would be relevant to our survey of Albee's **themes** to point out aspects of Purdy's work which attracted Albee to the story. This latter point is especially interesting, since Albee has stated that his main purpose in adapting the book was to introduce Purdy's work to a broader segment of the American public.

The greatest reason for the failure of Albee's adaptation is that the over-all production had gotten completely out of hand. The play has two acts, each with nine scenes plus several entre-scenes in which the main character, Malcolm, returns to the golden bench to speak with Professor Cox. In sum, there are too many scene changes required, too much interruption in the action, for the audience to maintain a deep interest. The play was so complex that the huge Schubert Theater was engaged, a theater normally used for elaborate musical productions. In addition to sheer mechanics, the play is a bizarre array of Absurdist scenes and characters which make the play an undigestible potpourri which attempts to convey a serious message, but is lost in maze - there is simply too much there.

The major **theme** of the story is the corruption of innocence, of the initiation of a young, untouched boy of fourteen or fifteen into the evil realities of life. Malcolm is an orphaned lad who in waiting for his father on a golden bench, comes into contact with an evil figure, Professor Cox, who proposes to introduce Malcolm to his "friends". What ensues is a myriad of characters and settings which demonstrate in a caricatured manner the "facts of life" - a soured marriage, greed, deceit, homosexual seduction, prostitution, etc. Perhaps the central failing of the play is the character of Malcolm himself, whose supposed innocence comes across as dull incredulity or just simple stupidity. He is without intellectual resources or imagination and is led from one manipulating character to another without ever comprehending what it all means. Finally, he is exposed to a nymphomaniac who literally loves him to death. Malcolm's education has thus been completed and there is doubt as to whether he actually dies, or perhaps only completes the rite of passage into adulthood. Although every part of Malcolm's initiation fails dramatically, Purdy and Albee's intent is clear - to satirize modern society and to portray the plight of the innocent, unknowing and uninhibited spirit. The world which is depicted, although it is in principle a realistic one, becomes far too distorted into Absurdity; for example, every character in the play is in some way sexually abnormal: every male has either a blatant or strongly implied homosexual affection for Malcolm and every female displays some kind of aberration - a dominating drive, nymphomania, or an old woman's unmasked lust. Albee was understandably attracted to Purdy's work, not only because he considers it extremely worthy, but because both men are intent in pointing out to their respective audiences the decay of values and mores in modern American society. Albee has proven, however, that he can accomplish this task far more effectively through his own dramatic creativity.

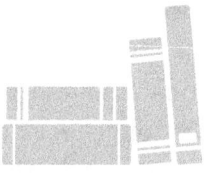

A DELICATE BALANCE

Nine months after the harsh reception accorded to *Malcolm*, Albee made an impressive comeback with a new, full-evening play, *A Delicate Balance*, which opened at the Martin Beck Theater on September 12, 1966. The play starred Jessica Tandy and Hume Cronyn as Agnes and Tobias. Criticism of the play was extremely mixed with at least one critic saying the play was better than *Who's Afraid of Virginia Woolf?* and another saying that it was an "old house" which had not been very skillfully redecorated. Some people felt it was Albee's most beautiful, richly musical play, but then went on to point out serious flaws in characterization. Nevertheless, *A Delicate Balance* was awarded the Pulitzer Prize on May 1, 1967, perhaps as much for its own merit as for nearly a decade of service which Albee had contributed to the theater.

In a number of ways *A Delicate Balance* is a further working out of themes introduced in earlier plays and a **foreshadowing**, at least to some extent, of Albee's latest play, *All Over*. The play might well be story of George and Martha a decade or more after we saw them in *Who's Afraid of Virginia Woolf?* The play appropriately takes place in the fall of the year since the characters, Tobias and Agnes, Harry and Edna, are in the later part of middle age. They have lost all the fire and prowess in marital combat which George and Martha so vigorously displayed.

Whatever intense emotional and sexual relationship may have existed between them has long since passed. The tone of their lives is a steady, dull one, in which they have accommodated and adjusted to reality in order to be able to establish a routine; however, beneath this surface calmness and complacency, there still runs a current of desperation and madness at the prospect of reality, which was closer to the surface in *Who's Afraid of Virginia Woolf?* The "delicate balance" on which this steady existence depends is closely parallel to the spiritual state of Julian in *Tiny Alice*, and quite as tenuous. Brother Julian had once lost his faith and momentarily his ability to function in society and for him, undoubting faith is the illusion which he uses to shield himself from external reality and from the reality of his own state of existence. He has regained his balance, but it is "delicate" and may someday send him over the precipice into madness. The action of *A Delicate Balance* is a descent into the emotional core of the home of Tobias and Agnes, in order to lay bare its true state, the purpose it serves, and the "delicate balance" which it sustains in making existence possible for its members.

    The confrontation action of the play, occurring in the night hours of a twenty-four hour period in a well-appointed home, centers around demands that are made on Tobias and Agnes' protective home routine by three outsiders who have come seeking shelter from their own great fears which have made theme unable to function independently. They are Harry and Edna, the couple's closest friends, and their hysterical daughter Julia. Through the demands these people make and the crisis which is generated, Albee develops several closely related themes. First, one of the more obvious concerns of the play is the nature of friendship and the limits to which it can be pushed, the demands one party of that bond has the right to make on the other. The close friendship between the two couples is stretched to the breaking point and is finally shattered when Harry and Edna abruptly threaten the "safe" routine of Tobias and Agnes' household. Duty to friends and the jealous desire for privacy and an isolated, non-committed existence come into painful conflict. It is, of course, a very simple request which the visitors make and requires no dramatic sacrifice, save exposure.

Julia, their daughter who is fast approaching middle-age, also arrives after the failure of her fourth marriage. To her, the heart is womb to which she can withdraw rather than facing the reality of her womanhood and her responsibility in helping her marriage to work. It is made clear that Julia has a long history of being unable to cope with her marital failures and her pilgrimage home after each failure becomes a painful, pathetic ritual for Tobias and Agnes. Julia's arrival is especially a great burden for Tobias because it seems to bring the painful remembrance that he has failed her as a father. It appears that Tobias has withdrawn into himself long ago, when both his daughter and his wife had needed him. Given this insight into his past, we realize that the question Tobias is facing is whether or not he can afford not to respond to these new demands. His long story of the cat he had many years ago, similar to Jerry's parable about his dog in *The Zoo Story*, makes clear the crisis with which he is confronted. When his cat suddenly ended its affection toward him, he did not have the patience to win it back, to give sufficiently of his love when it was needed and when it was being tested. But this, we learn, is the story of his life - a long history of withdrawing from reality in times of crisis which began when he was a young man and has continued through years of marriage. He has failed his daughter during the years when she was growing up and she is now too emotionally maladjusted to have a child or function in a marriage; he took a mistress when his wife needed him after their son died and then he refused to try to have another child for fear of exposing himself to another loss. Now Harry and

Edna intrude into his stable but shallow life and the temptation to turn them away is pressing.

The challenge also extends to Agnes, who values their routine just as highly. She is the stoic, silent bearer of an unhappy and lonely marriage, and it is she who introduces the possibility of losing her balance and going mad. Agnes is the "fulcrum" of their tranquil home, the one who bears the bitter memories of the past which Tobias seems to have forgotten, at least until their visitors arrive. But unlike the Mommy figure of Albee's early plays, Agnes is quite willing and indeed insists that Tobias make the decision of whether they can stay. Confronted then with the pressure of his own fear and guilt, his weakness, and Agnes' expectations, he is forced into a dramatic confrontation with self - and he finally allows Harry and Agnes to stay, indeed, he cannot afford for them to leave.

Thus in addition to testing the strength of friendship and of the hearth, Albee again returns to the **theme** of the need to face reality. He makes it clear in this case that retreat from reality and from the needs of others is far more destructive than facing up to those external demands, even though they may present unpleasantness and disruption of daily routine. This confrontation, which takes place in the night, brings so-called "demons" into the open, as it did in *Who's Afraid of Virginia Woolf?* and what is again demonstrated is that man still retains the ability to act. Tobias was able to overcome his human weakness, perhaps for the first time in his life, and in doing so became as admirable a man as Albee has yet to create.

Tobias differs from George in *Who's Afraid of Virginia Woolf?* because he was not swept into a highly abstract, symbolic destruction of illusion, but acted at a moment of specific need; thus, he is much more of an Everyman in the modern sense, who is quite unheroic, but becomes heroic in a modest way by making the decision to respond to a neighbor. What is in question, however, is the strength of Albee's affirmation in this renewal for love and commitment to one's fellow man. Agnes is prompt to announce the morning and gives the reassurance that they will soon forget what has taken place and will be able to return to their precious routine and its inherent isolation. Tobias, although he has proven himself worthy in a moment of crisis, has not developed the courage to change the quality of his life, to openly acknowledge his failures. Also there is no indication that in the future he will again succeed in affirming his humanity. Albee, at best, can only offer the hope that he will retain the potential.

One criticism of *A Delicate Balance* is that Albee never develops the reasons why Harry and Edna arrive in the first place. What is the unnamable "fear" they both experienced and why do they leave as abruptly as they came? Both characters have been described as "wooden" because they simply provide a convenient pretext for Tobias' confrontation and this, one critic said, is a "cop-out". But it has also been correctly pointed out that Albee deliberately chose to focus on Tobias and Agnes in order to study their response to this external demand. The fear of Harry and Edna, therefore, is not the center of concern as it might be in T. S. Eliot's *Sweeney Agonistes* or *The Family Reunion*. It is, on one level at least, the fear of getting old and of being able to watch oneself drift helplessly closer to the end and thus it would be expected to appear in late middle age. But more specifically, however, it is the familiar existential fear of Nothingness, in the words of Karl Jaspers, "the darkness in which the individual finds himself ... from his sense of forlornness when he stares without love into the void"; or of Eliot, "When you're alone in the middle of the night and you wake in a sweat and a hell of a fright" - in sum, an awareness of one's total nonessentiality and of one's alienation from humanity. It is this substrate of horror which affects the apparently secure characters in *The Family Reunion*, but which appears without notice in moments of apparent tranquility. Rather than developing this angle and thus jeopardizing the originality of his play, Albee has probed the responses of friends when the frightened couple seek shelter from this spectre. What is revealed, of course, is that Tobias and Agnes are vulnerable to the same fears and the "delicate balance" they so carefully maintain is also designed to protect them against that same spectre. The "bad night" which is experienced by all four characters displays the tremendous weakness of men and women who choose to isolate themselves rather than seek and give love. Whereas the old couple in Ionesco's *The Chairs* seek escape from the unnamed fear by committing suicide, Albee holds that the only hope for salvation lies in man's becoming a "communal nation."

As we mentioned earlier, *A Delicate Balance* has often invited comparison with *Who's Afraid of Virginia Woolf?*, not only for their closely related **themes** and basic setting, but also for the inadequacy of their minor characters. Like Nick and Honey, Harry and Edna play an important part in the development of the main conflict, but they are poorly drawn and appear far too functional. For the most part they are silent throughout the play, but when they do actively engage in the proceedings, they are far less convincing than Tobias and Agnes. Another rather questionable character is Claire, Agnes' alcoholic sister. She is present throughout the play delivering well-placed acerbic comments about what is taking place and she appears to have a drunkard's wisdom and an understanding of what is happening, but she is totally unable to help herself. Although she is rather pleasant and informative and does no real harm to the play, it appears that she has been inserted into the drama rather than having been woven into the play's fabric. One rather harsh judgment that might be made is that perhaps Albee simply wanted to include an alcoholic in one of his plays in order to round out the list of characters seen thus far who have sought refuge in different types of illusions.

Despite weaknesses in characterization and passages of language which are not among Albee's best, *A Delicate Balance* demonstrates a richness of maturity and persevering conviction in the worth of man that makes it an extremely worthy play and certainly one of Albee's best.

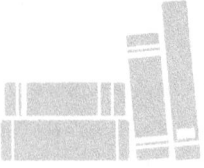

EVERYTHING IN THE GARDEN

Albee's third adaptation continued his unfortunate practice of alternating his major original plays with adaptations, a practice which he has hopefully stopped. *Everything in the Garden*, a play by the English writer Giles Cooper, opened on November 16, 1967 at the Plymouth Theater and starred a potential money-making team of Barbara Bel Geddes and Barry Nelson, who had been together in *Mary, Mary* and *The Moon is Blue*. Although the play is far better than *Malcolm*, it still received generally unfavorable critical and audience response. Critics again objected to the shallowness and lack of true dramatic genius in the composition.

Again, however, the **theme** of the play is pertinent to Albee's social vision and his primary purpose in adapting it was in Americanizing the setting and mechanical elements to make them more recognizable. *Everything in the Garden* is an examination of the typical middle-class family existing today in both England and America - the suburban, materialistic family who strive to live on a plane slightly above their means and who live the dream that they will eventually be able to afford additional signs of affluence. But what lies at the heart of this ostensibly decent and moral family, in the view of Cooper and Albee, is the secret greed and sheer thirst for money which could potentially be released at a moment of strong temptation.

The emergence of such an opportunity provides the dramatic pretext of the play's action as Albee turns these subliminal desires into a "business" proposition advanced by the mysterious Mrs. Toothe. Jenny, the middle-class housewife, secretly turns to a part-time job in Mrs. Toothe's "agency" and soon earns a substantial amount of money. Her husband Richard discovers her disgusting occupation and several melodramatic scenes of moral outrage follow. As the developments of the play get rather out of hand and we are informed that most of the neighborhood wives are engaged in the same pursuit with their husbands' cognizance, the play becomes a morality tale which proceeds to indict the hypocrisy of middle-class morals. In sum, the play is an interesting enough story, but fails to achieve the stature of true drama.

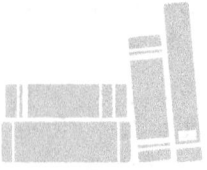

BOX-MAO-BOX

....

Albee's two one-act plays, *Box* and *Quotations from Chairman Mao Tse-Tung*, depart radically from his previous work and, indeed, from what we know as the theater in general. Rather than the highly dramatic, often explosive drama of confrontation through the various kinds of conflicts between characters which Albee has created in the past, he has here attempted a daring theatrical experiment utilizing a new kind of dramaturgy which is intended to reflect the immediate, day-to-day state of man's existence in society; it does not depend on conventional audience responses for its effect, but demands from them total passivity. The two plays together are called *Box-Mao-Box* because in the middle of the first play, Mao breaks in and continues for a time, until Box takes up again and the two proceed simultaneously to a unified conclusion.

The abrupt change in technique which this play represents and the nature of the play itself is difficult to describe in a brief discussion. The first thing to be aware of, however, is that Albee turns completely from conventional dramatic characterization, linear story development, and a long-running examination of the American family unit. He adopts instead a broader-based, more abstract and for more apocalyptic social commentary. Perhaps the single greatest impetus behind the play's form and its **theme** is the popularized work of Marshall McLuhan dealing with the effect on man and his environment of the mass proliferation of electronic data with which man is surrounded. It is a post-Absurdist, neo-Kafkaesque realization about the effects of the computer age. To make man aware of the changes which have taken place both in society and in the quality of his existence, Albee has created a play which is itself inspired by those changes, and seeks to protest and warn man against the dangers involved in not being able to retain a firm control of one's sensibilities in the midst of an electronic maze. As we shall note, the play achieves a total integration of form and content in which, to reflect the famous McLuhanism, the medium becomes the message - or at least in Albee's play it becomes as major part of the message.

The play opened first at the Studio Arena Theater in Buffalo, New York on March 6, 1968 and later, after changes were made in the script, at the Billy Rose Theater in New York City on September 30, 1968. Albee's note in the program, which was later reprinted in the published edition of the play, gave an important indication of the convictions which prompted this new experiment. He said first that the artist must seek to make a significant statement about man and, if at all possible, attempt to bring about change or improvement in society - art becomes a creative, reformist cultural force; second, the artist's obligation extends to the art form - to make it reflect the constant flux of the society which he addresses and speaks about. Thus Albee delivers a call for innovation in art, as he has often done, and an awareness of change in society. As might be expected, however, the critics were not impressed with Albee's experiment for the sake of change and for his plea for an open-minded consideration of the play. Critical response was almost uniformly negative and at least one reviewer called the play simple "trash" while others made only scant efforts to explain the play to their readers.

The first of the two plays, *Box*, contains no characters or stage props save a large transparent cube which is suspended from the ceiling; it is perfectly immobile. There is a single voice in the play which emits not from the cube, but from the back and sides of the theater; it is intended to surround the audience in sound and to diffuse their focus from what they normally see on the stage in front of them. The female voice which fills the hall, emitting from hidden speakers, is of a pleasant, smooth quality with no identifiable characterization intended; nor is it an institutional voice heard over intercoms in hospitals or office buildings - it is simply a human voice. The entire substance of the play consists of her long monologue - long rambling phrases alternated with short groups of sentences. At first it sounds disjointed, but the effect of a seemingly haphazard delivery is to gradually produce a deliberate cadence, the effect of which is to slowly involve the audience in the rhythm.

In a true sense the monologue the voice delivers is a lament, an elegiac dirge marking the passing away of the best aspects of our civilization. Critic Jack Kroll has probably come closest in identifying the voice as the lone surviving voice of sanity or even of life after a devastating holocaust. The monody laments the fact that man's most precious possession, his art, is passing away, decaying. Even simple things, like amateur craftsmanship, are becoming extinct and man is losing his innate creativity in a philistine Wasteland - there is no morality or celebration of the life spirit possible in the "global village" of electronic data. The voice which describes this sterility gives no indication of any specific international conflicts or participants who may have caused this decimation; however, the crucial fact is that it did occur and Albee makes it clear that there is a real possibility that such a thing could happen to us. The transparent cube, as Kroll said, becomes the coffin for our species, for our "flesh and spirit."

This is certainly Albee's most apocalyptic examination of the state of man's existence, and the hope which he has consistently been able to express is limited in this play to a single gull which flies away from the death net into which all the others meet their destruction. This lone gull represents, possibly, a glimmer of hope that man will yet make a conscious choice in changing his life; or, it could represent the imagination (as Poe sees birds representing it) and the possibility that art will not die in the sterile world of computers. This glimmer of hope, however, can be too easily overlooked in the dark picture which Albee draws of civilization.

As we mentioned earlier, the form of the play is an important part of the play's message - the disembodied voice is a reflection of the tremendous proliferation of data which is not only conveyed through the printed media, but also through the air waves - we are literally inundated with sound which is conveying what has become meaningless information. In being aware of this phenomenon of modern life, Albee has adopted a dramaturgy which relies totally on the audience's auditory perception and sensibility -the total sound and the total absence of visual spectacle necessitate a total concentration on what is said and therefore, as it has been pointed out, the action of the play takes place in the minds of the audience. Of course, this extraordinary demand on the viewer, who comes to the theater expecting a combination of sight and sound cues to enable him to "make sense" out of the play, caused the generally poor reception and uniform lack of understanding - audiences were not prepared to willingly suspend their intellectualizing of a play. Nevertheless, this radical alteration of art form was meant to reflect not only the flux of society, but also to underscore the objection of the alienated artistic spirit.

The second play appears at first to be quite different in both form and content from the preceding one, yet it becomes apparent that it is a closely related movement in a kind of musical composition. *Quotations from Chairman Mao Tse-Tung* contains four characters - an Old Woman, a Long-Winded Lady, a Minister, and Chairman Mao. Throughout the action of the play, which consists of pure recitation, there is a musical arrangement of the three voices (the Minister never speaks) which blend together to form a musical effect. Chairman Mao recites from the now famous *Red Book of Quotations*, the Long-Winded Lady rambles on at great length and the Old Woman repeats the opening lines of a poem - all of which is blended together with a great deal of precision, since the stage directions call for the speeches to be delivered with metronomic timing, with ellipses and dashes carefully interspersed throughout the text in order to indicate the orchestration of the voices. The scene of the play is the deck of an ocean liner, but there is no plot whatsoever, no destination or purpose for the trip and no relationship between the characters. Given three different types of people, three types of speech, the orchestrated effect is composed of three types of message: Mao delivers a series of what are now platitudes about the glory of Communism and the inevitable disintegration of the capitalistic and imperialistic systems; the Old Lady recites a poem entitled "Over the Hill to the Poorhouse"; and the Long-Winded Lady relates a number of stories about her sex life, an accident she witnessed and the death which followed, etc.

The final part of the experiment begins when the single voice in Box joins the three voices of Mao - each of the voices contributes its own message as the audience is inundated with total sound and, according to Albee, the only way for this data to have its intended effect, is to allow it to be taken in and then be acted upon by the unconscious. What is produced, in the words of one critic, is a "non-narrative polyphony of symbolism" -

extremely complex, contrapuntal sound texture - which makes sense only when viewed in sum, like the "colors on a painter's canvas."

Given these clues for comprehension, then what does the play mean? First of all, each character in the plays delivers an independent message, unrelated to the others which is intended to register in the minds of the audience and, if not summarily rejected as incomprehensible, be assimilated into a meaningful realization. Thus there are four streams of meaning. The box laments the demise of art, of simple creativity, of man's imagination in a world overwhelmed by the threat of a nuclear holocaust and by electronic proliferation of meaningless data. The Long-Winded Lady speaks about the total meaninglessness of her life and of her inability to comprehend the death she witnessed in the automobile accident. This loss of sensitivity is, of course, the result of watching the television screen night-after-night and seeing the dead and wounded being carried out of the jungles of Vietnam, or Biafra; or from watching hundreds of hours of war movies and violence of every conceivable nature - we have simply lost the ability to comprehend mass death and, in essence, we cannot differentiate a war movie from a newscast from Vietnam. This woman, perhaps more than any of Albee's other characters, is a typical product of modern life, of the "media explosion" which so many people have celebrated. Ironically enough, she speaks to the clergyman who is obviously bored and inattentive; he reflects the critical view of the Church which Albee has expressed before - he is unwilling or unable to console or to instill a lost awareness into the inhabitants of the modern world. The Old Lady is no doubt indicative of the wretched and purposeless existence which old people lead in our country and she is perhaps the echo of the vibrant Grandma we saw in *The Sandbox* - now however, she has nothing to look forward to except the poorhouse or an old-age home. The people who have not reached her age have become insensitive to the old and they simply attempt to push them aside. Another great "conscious unawareness" or self-lie is represented by Chairman Mao, who walks throughout the theater delivering his message of revolution: Here Albee intends a **satire** of American foreign policy and also of the common man's refusal to accept the reality of Communist China. Although this specific aspect of the message is now somewhat dated in view of recent foreign policy developments, it has long been a major puzzlement that our government should maintain an official unawareness of that regime.

Thus there are four major inputs of data which are intended to flow into the unconscious of the viewer and ideally be assimilated into a meaningful realization. What is this realization? It is primarily that the world is changing, generally not for the better, while the American public is not changing. We are, in effect, allowing ourselves to be overwhelmed with reality and consequently we are losing ground in our battle against the huge electronic, computerized machine. Albee is therefore calling for awareness - not only of political realities, but also of the quality of our lives, of the fact that when art suffers, civilization is in terrible danger. But as in all of Albee's plays, the sole hope of survival is in man's retaining his ability to act and to affect his life. In this sense, the most important symbol of the entire work is the lone sea gull who turns away from the mammoth death net of the computerized world-machine and heads on an individual course.

The risk Albee took in mounting such a statement on a non-narrative, non-sequential dramatic structure and in depending on a musical orchestration of the thematic strands, was that the entire message could potentially remain unrecognizable to both critics and public who are very hesitant in accepting radical change. Nevertheless, the work is an impressive accomplishment, as well as being quite beautiful in its production. It is significant in terms of Albee's work because it not only affirms but also expands upon his social and artistic commitment to make his art a powerful tool in making man aware of the world in which he lives and of his own position in that world.

ALL OVER

Three years after *Box-Mao-Box*, Albee introduced a play which he intends to join with another play called *Seascape*; the two will be collectively entitled *Life and Death*. *All Over* opened at the Martin Beck Theater on March 27, 1971. The play was directed by Sir John Gielgud and the fine cast included Jessica Tandy as the Wife, Colleen Dewhurst as the Mistress, and George Voskovec as the Best Friend. Critical response to the play was primarily unfavorable, even though it received enthusiastic reviews from two leading critics who called it one of the most important American plays of "several seasons" and said it was "Lovely, poignant and deeply felt." Objections to the play were far from convincing - one critic said the language was "artificial" and another said it was full of "trumped up revelations". One stock objection which has been leveled against many plays, including *Waiting for Godot*, is that "nothing happens" in the play. Albee was both stunned and angered by the play's poor reception and took to the public media to voice his objections and to attack once again the state of American theatrical criticism, something he has done several times in interviews and in *Fam and Yam*. The point of this criticism is simply that he considers the critics to be far too arbitrary and incompetent and that it is unfortunate that they possess the power literally to "make or break" a play.

In *All Over* Albee has departed from the highly abstract, experimental structure of *Box-Mao-Box* and returned to a basically naturalistic setting. However, one can easily detect the impact of the previous play and be aware of the fact that this is one of his most innovative plays. Albee has continued throughout his career to experiment and learn and also to accept the risk of not always succeeding. *All Over* is a great artistic success because, as we shall discuss, the playwright has created a tremendously rich and complex texture which is comparable in beauty to that of *Who's Afraid of Virginia Woolf?* Another important aspect of the play is that it provides a clear indication of the direction in which Albee has been headed in the past decade. As we have already seen in this chronological survey of his work, Albee has repeatedly returned to the family unit or, perhaps more accurately, to an examination of relationships between people and the ways in which people both hurt and love. He began with the Absurdist Mommy and Daddy in *The Sandbox* and *The American Dream*, took a far more intensified view in *The Death of Bessie Smith* and *Who's Afraid of Virginia Woolf?* and after the bitter scene in *The Ballad of the Sad Café*, he turned to a more mellow portrayal in *A Delicate Balance*. Although each of these plays deals with many important **themes** in addition to the love relationship between people, they are based on that central concern. Albee has, in effect, been studying the process of living in society and having to deal with deeply personal needs and with the demands of the external world.

In *All Over* the battles, illusions, fantasies, **black humor**, lies, private crimes and petty disappointments have faded into the past and become painful memories, as both the characters and the playwright face the very real prospect of human mortality. What emerges from this long, probing study is that the world Albee sees is quite an unhappy one and is filled with imperfection and failure and that the temptation to escape is always present. Those alternatives have disappeared in *All Over* - the play is a confrontation with finality and a time for a backward and inward look at how one has spent a lifetime.

As the play opens we are informed that a man is dying, an extremely wealthy and famous man. Members of his family and his closest friends have gathered to wait for the end: his Wife, from whom he had long been separated; his Mistress, with whom he had spent many years; his son and daughter; his Best Friend; and the old family physician. There is no action in the play save the slow ebbing of life, charted by the doctor's periodic reports, and the man's death. The entire play is a series of revelations and reminiscences about each of the main characters' lives - events, motivations, desires, disappointments, etc., all of which creates a living portrait of past and present. From the Wife and Mistress, who are contraposed throughout the play, we gain a full account of the factors that have led up to their present positions as estranged wife and devoted lover. The Wife, we learn, has always been somewhat like Agnes of *A Delicate Balance* - solid, devoted, loyal and completely unexciting. Mistress, on the other hand, has spent a lifetime of romantic encounter, giving fully of a gay and sensual personality. The Wife is bitter, her life has been one of self-pity and anger at the turn her marriage took and at the extreme disappointment in not being the kind of woman her husband seems to have found so attractive. But the infuriating thing which eats at her is the fact that she loves her husband and yet has never been able or even willing to attempt a reunion. Living reminders of her bitterly disappointing life are her son and daughter, both of whom she despises. They have obviously suffered from their mother's hate and their father's dashing, romantic love life - the daughter is filled with outrage at everything which takes place, she is loud and unsatisfied, much in the mold of Martha in *Who's Afraid of Virginia Woolf?* She has married unhappily and, quite typically, is childless. The son is totally ineffectual, almost effeminate. He expresses his emotions by childish nostalgia for little things, like the room of the house in which he used to live, and is never far from tears. The spectacle of the wife and her emotionally crippled children is one of the saddest pictures Albee has created. It is the living result of a wasted and selfish life.

Although the mistress' life has been spent in the pursuit of and giving of happiness, it is clear that she has never produced anything permanent - neither a marriage, nor children. With the death of her lover she is left only with memories and the frightening prospect of loneliness. Her life has also been wasted and basically selfish, since she never saw fit to give anything but ephemeral, romantic love. Thus the **theme** of the play is the two-sided coin of selfishness and waste. These characters have lived their lives without ever producing or creating anything lasting and wholesome and thus they are failures. Albee demonstrates that the unhappiness of man in the world, despite the uncertainty and unpleasantness of reality, is ultimately of his own doing. Albee places a heavy burden on man - that of his own freedom to act, and when he errs for the sake of selfishness and his own weakness, he must bear the consequence, which is really the final realization of a wasted life.

The most outstanding accomplishment of the play is its structure - the precise orchestration of language which works together to create a rich verbal texture. We saw in discussing *Box-Mao-Box* that Albee developed the play by using a non-sequential, non-narrative text which was intended to have the effect of a musical composition. *All Over* is quite similar in that each character, although he is involved with the others, delivers or perhaps executes his speeches to achieve an orchestrated effect. In other words, the dialogue is not that of the naturalistic interplay of previous plays, but a precisely mapped and cadenced delivery which fits together into a meaningful whole. There is purposely no action in the play because, as in *Box-Mao-Box*, the action is designed to take place in the unconscious of the audience.

    Thus it seems likely that the play was not widely appreciated precisely because it was not designed to operate in the same way as a conventionally naturalistic drama. The play consists primarily of a series of confrontations within each individual and whatever central unifying focus there is, is intended to be the larger framework for the individual realizations. Hopefully Albee will continue in the development of this technique and it will have an impact on other playwrights. This seems preferable to accommodating art to popular taste.

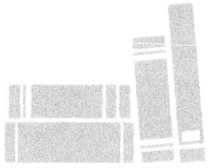

WHO'S AFRAID OF VIRGINIA WOOLF?

CRITICAL ANALYSIS OF WHO'S AFRAID OF VIRGINIA WOOLF?

INTRODUCTION

The success of *Who's Afraid of Virginia Woolf?* was the key to Albees's entry into the first ranks of American playwrights. Ironically, through the great financial success of the play, he also became a prominent figure in the financial quarter of the American Theater Establishment, an institution he has so often criticized. Nevertheless, Albee proved to producers and financial backers that a straight, full-length dramatic work could still be a huge success and thus extremely profitable. *Who's Afraid of Virginia Woolf?* both shocked and thrilled the audiences who become entranced with the play's powerful language and incredible displays of marital cruelty. Some people could not abide Martha's obscene, grating language - one member of the Pulitzer Prize Selection Committee called it simply a "filthy play." Another reviewer compared it to a "sewer overflowing."

Although the play received generally enthusiastic notices, not everyone was agreed on its meaning: some said it was simply a "dissection of an extremely ambiguously sick marriage"; but another found it to be strictly a "political play" and specifically, a "political allegory". One reviewer, who was clearly in the minority, said it was about "four homosexuals" masquerading as heterosexual couples; or, as another said, George and Martha are clearly meant to be George and Martha Washington.

Despite some confusion about what Albee was trying to "say" in the play, *Who's Afraid of Virginia Woolf?* was a great success and, as we have seen in our chronological review, it was widely performed. It remains to this date Albee's overall best work and has become one of the major works of contemporary drama.

What more can be said about the play, however, other than it is about a "sick marriage"? Is the play a political allegory? And what does the title mean? Albee has told us that he first saw the phrase "Who's afraid of Virginia Woolf?" written on a graffiti wall in a Greenwich Village bar. How does the play relate to the major **themes** of Albee's drama and does it fulfill the major premise of confronting the audience with a realistic picture of the condition of man? How are the principles of confrontation specifically applied? In order to answer these questions as well as others which will arise, we should first analyze in detail both the action and the characterization.

SIGNIFICANCE OF SETTING AND CAST

By setting the action in the living room of a middle-class home, Albee indicates he is analyzing a domestic relationship in the arena where the family reveals itself by "socializing" on its own terms.

The professional relations among the members of the cast are by their very nature potentially dramatic: George is a middle-aged history professor in a college where his father-in-law is president! This puts George in an unusually ambiguous relation to both his employer and his wife Martha; and it puts Martha in a position emphasizing the matrilineal heritage of power. Note too that George specializes in history, while their guest Nick teaches biology: Albee is ironically showing us the kinds of people who can legitimately be entrusted with studying man's social and biological growth!

Finally, the fact that Nick and Honey are a younger couple than their hosts promises a kind of double-exposure of married life in academe: both at its outset and in its fulfillment.

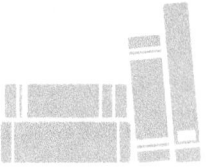

WHO'S AFRAID OF VIRGINIA WOOLF?

TEXTUAL ANALYSIS

ACT ONE: FUN AND GAMES

GEORGE AND MARTHA'S ENTRANCE

The audience's first sight of George and Martha sets the tone of the entire play and immediately characterizes the general state of their marriage. Note the dramatic functions of Martha's accusation that George is a do-nothing and a failure: suspense has been created because we shall now want to see whether Martha is justified in her accusation. Also, even though we do not realize it now, her accusation has introduced **irony** into the play because of the action which George finally does take. With this first note of Martha's loud aggressiveness, the conflict of the play begins to unfold.

ARRIVAL OF GUESTS

Technically speaking, the initial moment (Freytag's "irregendes Moment") of the drama is sprung with George's warning Martha not to talk about their son to the guests. This increases suspense, introduces the major ground of conflict, and heightens the mystery of the characters' lives. The brief exchange of niceties when the guests appear reveals, first of all, that Honey's social graces seem to be the extent of her ability to engage in intelligent conversation. Also, we witness the first dramatic contrast between George and Nick. Note that Nick offers reserved comments while George replies with sharp comments and petty contradictions. This preliminary confrontation serves to set Nick on the defensive.

In the first few moments of the play, then, Albee has established several important facts essential to later action. The opening moments characterize George and Martha: George allegedly has never done anything and so Martha is full of resentment and hostility; their usual means of communication, even when they are not discussing any serious issue, is through exchange of acerbic comments punctuated with insulting remarks; and it is (suspensefully) important to George that their son be kept a secret from their guests. The first meeting of the two couples also introduces and characterizes the younger Nick and Honey as polite enough but quite reserved - especially Nick; here Albee also establishes one of the elements of later conflict - George is more cynical and adept at language than Nick and succeeds in putting Nick on a permanent alert.

NICK AND GEORGE'S CONVERSATION

With the ladies out of the room, the conflict between the men is developed to reveal a fundamental contrast in personality. The dialogue makes it clear that Nick's only real concern is to succeed academically: little else seems to matter to him. And note that when George discusses his own "dashed hopes and good intentions" in his own career at the college, he verifies for the audience Martha's charge that he is a donothing. George's failure is of course in sharp contrast to Nick's high hopes of quickly making his mark. Note again Albee's use of **irony** in this discussion of the nature of academic life: when George characterizes it as a life of "musical beds," he is speaking ironically because he says even more than he knows. And dramatic suspense is further intensified by the disproportionately serious response that George makes to Nick's almost routine inquiry about what could be assumed to be public knowledge: whether George and Martha have children. George's reply is mystifying and crucial to the play's development: "That's for me to know and you to find out." Is this a real challenge or is it simply part of George's cynical humor intended further to antagonize Nick? Note that Albee compounds our confusion by not allowing us to linger on such puzzlements: he has George direct the conversation back to university life.

This first of two major confrontations between George and Nick is significant, then, for two reasons: it develops the conflict between George's cynicism and Nick's reserved earnestness, and the contrast between George's rationalization of failure and Nick's undaunted ambition; and it provides deeper insight into the reasons behind Martha's discontent with George, reasons dramatically supplied by George himself.

MARTHA AND HONEY RETURN

Notice that Albee's entrances and exits do not simply move the characters around for subsequent action, they advance the action on a higher level. Thus Honey's return has the dramatic function of notifying the audience of Martha's divulgence to Honey that Martha and George have a son. Note too that the dramatic announcement - which in itself is a real present event - is then followed by a symbolic reminiscence (Martha's recollection of how she once accidentally knocked George down in a mock boxing match) and a symbolic present event (George's firing at Martha with a gun that proves to be a pop-gun) with strong Freudian implications. In other words, Albee manages to achieve his characterizations in depth by using significant free associations and acted-out fantasies. It becomes apparent through the boxing story that Martha knows precisely what George's vulnerabilities are and this becomes her first step in using such personal information against him. The shooting of the toy gun with its loud noise and its ejection of a parasol instead of a bullet achieves comic relief through surprise and incongruity. And it heightens the characterizations of the hosts: for even though George has attempted to seize the center of attention and to dramatize his anger at Martha, she still has the final word when, with one remark to Nick, she turns George's "gun" into a symbol of his own weak manhood and simultaneously achieves a contrast in character by suggesting that Nick does not need such "props."

SECOND ROUND OF CONVERSATION

In this second sustained burst of dialogue and action, Albee achieves another dramatic contrast in terms of the development of two story lines: Nick's expounding of his plans to create a population of genetically perfect men stands in dramatic opposition to Martha's anecdotes about her husband and her son which add up to an account of man's cycle of rise and fall. Nick's ambitions are visionary, futuristic, idealistic, abstract; Martha's saga of failure is personal, historical, real, and all too human. Note too that George's second symbolic act repeats the essence of the first: his smashing a bottle against the bar is just as impotent an act as was the pop-gun murder-pantomime. The audience by now is encouraged to engage in thinking on several levels by George's singing of the **parody** of the nursery **rhyme**: "Who's Afraid of Virginia Woolf?" The substitution of the name of a permanent feminist for "the big bad wolf" begins to take on cumulative significance at this point in the action.

This final scene of Act One seems to round out the characterization. Nick seems idealistic to the point of relative unconcern with the present and the actual. George is a sympathetic figure who seems trapped in a marriage with a domineering woman who seeks to humiliate him at every opportunity. As the first act ends, George appears to be a sad and defeated man.

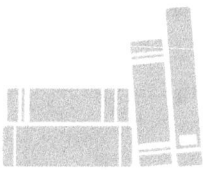

WHO'S AFRAID OF VIRGINIA WOOLF?

TEXTUAL ANALYSIS

ACT TWO: WALPURGISNACHT

....

SECOND CONVERSATION BETWEEN GEORGE AND NICK

The structure of the play now becomes more apparent as the two men are alone for the second time. Revelations of character and of man's condition are repeatedly made through contrasts and spontaneous free associations. And, as in the first conversation between the two, very important fuel is supplied for further use when the entire company reassembles. Nick's startling and unsolicited divulgences about Honey's hysterical pregnancy and the fortune she received from her father reveal serious flaws in their supposedly ideal marriage and in Nick's supposedly idealistic view of life. Nick's confession at least causes a reappraisal of our conception of him and his wife. But what can we see as the dramatic function of George's equally unmotivated story about a young boy who accidentally shot his mother and then killed his father? Certainly it is a tragic story, it supplies the first really tender moments of the play, and in some way it obviously means a great deal to George, but we have no idea of its specific relevance to the immediate plot. (It is, however, brought into the play twice more and takes on an uncertain importance.) We could note, expecting contrast as we do by now, that George's story of a child who rejects his parents is quite the opposite of George's own dependence on the older generation! Certainly contrast emerges again in George's philosophical statement about the nature of civilization: Its alleged decay and inevitable demise, and George's belief in adjustment and accommodation as the principle of survival, all stand in sharp opposition to Nick's theory of genetic control and perfection.

HUMILIATE THE HOST

The action of the play now undergoes a qualitative change. The "fun and games" of the first act, which were merely a series of insults and disparaging anecdotes, now become savagely serious. This new "play" takes on the characteristic of a death game in which George's earlier symbolic enactment of assault becomes actual physical assault. Note that once again an entrance is actually a threat: just as Honey's first re-entrance brought shocking news of Martha's talk about their son, so now Martha's re-entrance delivers a bombshell in the form of her inquiry whether George has told Nick of his book about the boy and how "Daddy" prevented its publication. This "inquiry" indicates that either she was listening in on their conversation or that she knows George so well she has learned his habit of telling this story to anyone who has never heard it before. It is possible that the proceedings we witness in this scene have taken place before and that they follow a familiar pattern in which Martha succeeds in humiliating George before others. In any event, this new development finally characterizes George as a man who has failed to make his one single meaningful statement to the world. And there is an important note of dramatic ambiguity raised between George's tragic story of the boy and Martha's account of it: The boy in George's story had gone mad but Martha claims that the boy actually was George. Who is correct? Is George mad? Or is this story a fantasy with which he has identified? Or is it a story based partly on truth and partly fictionalized? Whatever the answer, Martha's new all-out psychological attack on George provokes him now not to impotent symbolic retaliation (as with the pop-gun and the bottle broken on the bar) but to actual physical counter-attack. Note how the symbolism of occupations figures again in the action: while George the realistic historian is driven to physical violence, Nick the idealistic biologist intervenes to preserve life. The rhythm of the action is now settled upon and sustained: revelation, attack, recoil, greater attack. We do not know as yet the extent to which this pattern will develop.

GET THE GUESTS

This scene is dramatically important for several reasons. There is a lull in the action which not only strengthens the play's fidelity to the ebb and flow of life but also increases the suspense. And the calm heightens the surprise development in character as George virtually takes over as a gamesmaster and in effect co-opts this kind of psychological weapon. His thinly veiled allegory about a wealthy heiress who got her man through a false pregnancy is of course based on what Nick had confided earlier. The action is becoming increasingly vicious: compare, for example, the initial slur on George in the boxing allegory with this present attack on the guests. This increase in vehemency combined with the overt formalizing of the game structure indicates that we are being drawn into a deadly vortex of cruelty. The specific function of the attack on the guests is that it places the two couples on an equal basis - now we know some dark secrets of each marriage. Significantly though, Martha has thus far escaped a specific attack in the games. This too increases the suspense. Has George used "Get the Guests" as a warm-up for an attack on Martha or as a way of delaying "Hump the Hostess"?

HUMP THE HOSTESS

Note that we sense that this is the climactic scene because each of the main characters is driven to employ what seems to be his ultimate weapon: Martha, her power to commit adultery; George, his power to influence life through fantasy, allegory, or fictionalizing. It is clear that Martha's express purpose in making sexual advances to Nick is to make George jealous and to further infuriate him. Perhaps his ignoring of this behavior spurs her on to an extreme that she might not have originally intended. Thus the action reaches a new peak of desperate fury: Martha's overt move toward adultery is the final blow to George's manhood and his angry reaction of throwing the book against the door-chimes is only a surface indication of the rage he has thus far endured. Is the throwing of the book another impotent gesture like the firing of the toy gun and the smashing of the bottle? Certainly we are led to keep that possibility in mind, and the fact that we do is evidence of Albee's finesse in characterization and dramatic timing. But immediately we see that this gesture is not one of impotent fury but rather one of calculated counter-attack: for we realize that now George is talking to Honey as if the sounding of the chimes has been caused by a messenger delivering a telegram announcing their son's death. For the first time (at the **climax** of the play) the audience can see clear disparity between fact and fiction. What does George's fabrication signify? What is the strange nature of their son that George first did not want Martha to mention him and that now George decides he is dead?

TITLE OF ACT TWO

We are now in a better position to appreciate the title of the second act: "Walpurgisnacht." This term refers to the belief of medieval peoples in Central and Western Europe that on Walpurgis Night, the eve of May Day, the evil power of the witches was at its greatest peak. Men of the villages would assemble after sunset and make banging noises to drive the witches away. The action of Albee's second act completes the full **exposition** of the "evils" which beset both marriages - frustration, deceit, false expectations, jealousy, rage, sexual antagonism, etc. - and in a ritualistic way makes these evils ready to be exorcised.

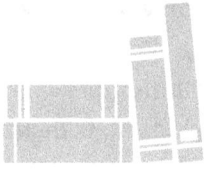

WHO'S AFRAID OF VIRGINIA WOOLF?

TEXTUAL ANALYSIS

ACT THREE: THE EXORCISM

HOUSEBOY

The ebb-and-flow pattern that we identified earlier is now dramatically emphasized. Martha's dejected entry, alone, her mood of exhaustion and self-disgust, are all in sharp contrast to her earlier frenzy. The new lull is needed as a respite by both characters and audience: this is the calm of insight, however bitter. This scene largely completes the ironic characterization of Nick and advances the character development of Martha. Her description of Nick as incapable of consummating the love act is the last step in our re-characterization of him from ostensible wonder-boy to phony, opportunistic fool. We appreciate again the **irony** in his occupation: the biology expert is himself incapable of reliable animal behavior! But Martha's demoting him to "Houseboy" contributes to her own characterization too: it underscores her tendency to choose men she can hold in contempt, perhaps even men that she can most easily reduce to contempt. The scene is now set for resolution of the many evils that have been exposed.

BRINGING UP BABY

This final "game" that George creates is, like most of the action, ironic, symbolic, and ritualistic. It is ironic because while George calls for Martha to review the "bringing up" of their son, the present action is really a rite of maturation for Martha and George - it is they who have been babies and who are now "bringing up" themselves under George's new leadership. The Latin prayers of the Requiem Mass, and the mournful poem "Dies Irae" which George recites, symbolize not only the death of their imaginary son but the death of their neurotic way of life, hence a ritualistic rebirth of themselves. Apparently the two of them have maintained the illusion of a son to compensate for Martha's never having had real children and to give their empty lives some content. The ritual of purgation which George undertakes represents not only the killing of the imaginary child but of all the evils exposed during the Walpurgisnacht. The characters have all been stripped of their pettiness, phoniness unwillingness to face the truth. George's long since forgotten challenge to Nick ("That's for me to know and you to find out") now takes on prophetic as well as ironic implications - neither Nick nor the audience imagined that such a fictitious creation existed nor that it would be exorcised in a ritual of Latin prayers culminating in the soft singing of the ironic nursery **rhyme**. The question in the title, in the parody-song, is now answered: it is the domineering Martha who is afraid of the "Woolf" and together with George she must now take that terrifying step into the existential void in which honest people re-create themselves.

Questions remain, however. What is the significance of the fact that George's account of the death of their "son" is identical to that of the death of the young boy's father in the story? Is the young boy really George? Was George's motive purely one of revenge? And what does all this add up to?

We have been exposed to a maze of ambiguities, bizarre rituals, symbolic acts, death enactments, an assault, and a full exploration of the seemingly hateful relationship between two emotionally sick people. And our task is to make sense of the action and to identify the major **themes** of the play.

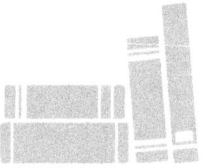

WHO'S AFRAID OF VIRGINIA WOOLF?

CHARACTER ANALYSIS

MARTHA

The initial insult Martha levels against George, "What a cluck you are," begins the strange spectacle of a duel between those two people which, although beginning in drunken revelry, becomes a play to the death. After reviewing the characterization in all of Albee's plays, it becomes clear that many aspects of Martha's outward behavior resemble those of Mommy in *The American Dream* and certainly of Nurse in *The Death of Bessie Smith*. All three women appear to be the stereotyped, dissatisfied female who constantly berates her mate for his overall inadequacy. As we have noted, however, Nurse is far more developed than Mommy - this is also true of Martha.

Martha is a middle-aged woman of fifty-two, six years older than George, a fact which infuriates her. She is well-educated but by no means refined - in fact, she is almost totally devoid of genuine feminine charm. Martha's abrasive and often obscene language and her unmasked sexual aggressiveness make her an extremely unpleasant person. Yet Martha is a complex character with important dimensions which differentiate her from the Absurdist Mommy figure and which give depth to her incredibly hostile behavior.

What are the causes of Martha's hostility toward George? The single reason we are given for her bitter dissatisfaction is that her married life has been nothing but years of disillusionment and frustration which have consequently soured her personality. She has spent years lamenting the fact that George has failed miserably in fulfilling the expectations that she held for him. In her mind, George has failed both as a husband and as a career educator - or at least failed in the sense he has not matched the formidable stature of her near-deified father, the president of New Carthage College. Of course, the expectations which she set for him were rather too idealistic: George was to rise steadily in the history department and then be groomed to eventually succeed her father and thus Martha's position as the leading lady of college social-life would be assured. However, as she has so emphatically and repeatedly informed us, George is "A flop!" and he constantly suffers in being compared with the old man.

At her frenetic best, Martha closely resembles a character from the naturalistic Strindbergian theater of sexual combat. In particular, she closely parallels the character Alice in Strindberg's play *The Dance of Death* (1901): she is dissatisfied with her husband, takes a lover, attempts to humiliate her husband, eventually becomes dissatisfied with her lover, taunts her husband for his inadequacy, etc. Also, like the Strindbergian antagonist seen throughout his plays, she is driven and controlled by an abnormal sexual desire which cannot be subdued through rational means. This character is committed to playing the game of "crush the husband" which is really a castration drive which seeks sexual fulfillment through the domination and humiliation of the male. Quite typically, however, she finds no satisfaction and remains unhappy and frustrated.

Such personality behavior is very apparent in Nurse and certainly in Martha. The humiliation drive describes precisely her treatment of George-she berates and belittles him for his inadequacy as a man and openly broadcasts stories about him which she feels are indicative of that inadequacy, the boxing **episode**, for example. What is most apparent, of course, is the steady stream of insults, verbal cruelty and violence which fill the confined atmosphere of the play. The ultimate weapon in this offensive is, of course, her adulterous conduct in which she appears to cuckold him practically in front of his eyes, but we are informed later that even here she could not obtain satisfaction because Nick failed to perform. It is Martha's constant occupation of attempting to both dominate and humiliate George which forms the basis for the dramatic conflict. The running game of one-upsmanship is what we are immediately confronted with and we have every reason to suppose that Martha's initial-entry remark is quite typical of life in their household.

However, the questions arise: Are there deeper causes involved in this dramatization of marital strife? Is there a greater depth to Martha than is immediately apparent?

As we have noted in discussing *The Death of Bessie Smith*, such extraordinarily abnormal behavior in savagely attacking the male is symptomatic of far more serious but less apparent failures. Though Martha is the dominant figure in the family unit, we discover in the third act of the play that she is the most vulnerable of all the characters. Although we cannot reach a certain conclusion until the final scene of the play, we realize that at the heart of this unhappy household is not the verbal game of insult and mutual recrimination, but something far more malignant: we become aware that Martha has lost sight of reality or, more accurately, that she has become unable to face reality and has built a life around the grand illusion of the make-believe son. The reality from which she hides is not only her disappointment in George, but also the emptiness of her life without ever having children (there are suggestions that both she and George are physically sterile). Her life and her marriage lack ultimate fulfillment and, made to depend solely on George for love, she found only imperfection. Therefore, she has retreated into illusion by creating the wish-fulfillment projection of the imaginary child and uses it to find meaning for her existence. But like all illusions, in Albee's view, it is at base only a sterile projection of a sterile imagination.

It is obvious that Martha is not a happy person. The illusion she sustains (with George's co-operation) may indeed give her some poor reason for living, but it cannot possibly bring the fulfillment which can only come in human contact. The only communication which occurs between Martha and George is the battle of insults which, as some critics have suggested, substitutes for the excited activity of sexual intercourse. But given the paradox that neither George nor the illusionary child can make her happy, the question must be asked: Does Martha detest George as much as her savage attacks would indicate? The conclusive answer to this comes in the third act immediately before George begins the final game of "Bringing Up Baby." Martha is visibly disgusted with herself and with the entire evening's events; she admits that George is the only "man in my life who has ever ... made me happy." Then in a tired voice, quietly sad, she says that it is George who is good to me, and whom I revile; ... who keeps learning the games we play as quickly as I can change the rules.

So we see that what appears to be her hate of George and a vicious attempt to humiliate him with every possible insult, takes on a new dimension. Although she loves George and he is the only one who ever made her happy or satisfied her sexually, it seems she cannot help but make him her partner in sado-masochistic games. She seems inwardly compelled to carry on activities, "games," which certainly do not give her satisfaction and are aimed at destroying the only person she loves. She is sick person to be sure, but what is the cause of these activities?

The answer to this lies in the very nature of the illusion which both she and George sustain. Although it does not bring her happiness, it is nevertheless the most precious thing in her life; and although she assumes a tough facade, the illusion is her greatest vulnerability. Thus the illusion is a paradoxical thing which she loathes for what it does to her and yet she cannot rid herself of it - this explains why the ritual George performs is both an exorcism of an evil and a Requiem for a beloved one who has died. Seen in these circumstances, the reason for her treatment of George is not only her frustration at his overall failings, but more specifically it arises from the rage she feels at George's failure to end the illusion, to take assertive action. She both loves George and is outraged at his failure to take her in hand. Thus what appears to be the callousness of a castrating virago, is the pained complaint of an unhappy and sick woman. But as with Nurse, the ultimate cause, for both her discontent and the illusion itself, is a spiritual failing grounded in an inability to find happiness or meaning in the world. Rather than seeking the comfort of human contact, she both partakes in and contributes to the pervasive sterility of society.

GEORGE

George, a history professor, is strongly but somewhat misleadingly characterized by Martha's detailed account of his many failures in both married and professional life. He is the constant target of her sharp-edged reproaches and elaborate, savage attacks. According to Martha, George's main difficulty is that he lacks aggressiveness and never does anything but "talk." Martha scorns George's bookishness, which she could never understand, and his cynical outlook. Seeing only failure and imperfection, she is seemingly engaged in destroying whatever is left of his manhood.

Like Martha, George is much more fully drawn than his counterpart (Daddy) in *The American Dream*, although both are dominated by their wives and intimidated for their inadequacy. George, however, is far more complex and as the play progresses, he visibly changes and finally becomes a fully developed and very engaging character. From the beginning, however, George is the most intelligent and sensitive of all the characters, a humanist who possesses a social consciousness of broad scope which has been enriched by life-long study of the actions and natures of men in the past. Unfortunately, such potential wisdom has been made ineffectual since he is quite as spiritually sterile and troubled as Martha. He is powerless to take any kind of effective action, least of all to put his own house in order. Nevertheless, he displays more perspective than any of the characters - especially Nick. As we have seen in our analysis of the action, George and Nick are diametrically opposed in their philosophical outlooks and George is prompt in pointing out the fallacies inherent in Nick's untempered faith in science and his simplistic view of success. He attempts to inform Nick of his errors and at the same time reveals a deep cynicism toward civilization in general and academic life in particular. For this wasted potential, but especially for the humiliation he suffers from Martha, the audience feels more compassion for him than for the other characters, least of all for the Martha of the first two acts.

It is difficult to say what caused George's lack of success in married and academic life. Certainly he was not given any real encouragement by being compared with Martha's father and invariably suffering in the comparison. In his first conversation with Nick, he reveals a number of rationalizations to account for his failure to become chairman of the history department, but these are, at best, unconvincing. Another more attractive possibility, however, is that his bitter cynicism toward academic life is at least partially justified and that he is simply an individualist who refused to "sell out" and play into the hands of Martha and her pompous father. We cannot, however, arrive at any definite conclusions because there are a number of puzzling aspects about George which are never clearly explained in the play. For example, what was George's role in the creation of the imagined child? Are we to believe that George was the young man in the novel who accidentally shot his mother and killed his father? Or, is this George's own fantasy and a failure to identify truth from illusion?

There are circumstances about his life, quite comparable to Martha's, which may have led to seek refuge in illusion - both that of Martha's child and the story of the young boy. It is reasonable to assume that George was also affected with loneliness and disappointment in not having children and that he too found imperfection and indifference when he sought to rely on Martha alone for emotional fulfillment. It is also quite possible that his career is so lack-luster because he simply does not have the requisites for fighting his way through the ranks - aggressiveness and sustained drive and even an adequate degree of brilliance.

Martha, in fact, may have been correct in characterizing him as nothing but a talker and never a doer - which prepares us precisely for the change which occurs between the second and third acts. But whatever the original reasons were for his becoming so cynical and ineffective in dealing with Martha, he is in the same emotional and spiritual condition - dependent on illusion, dissatisfied with his life and the people around him, yet trapped in the household in which there is constant torment and emotional chaos. He is totally unable to take any kind of action which would change the state of his existence.

George's story of the young boy presents an interesting note of ambiguity in the development of the plot and in the characterization. There are three revelations in the play which concern the young boy. First, George tells the boy's story to Nick not as something that happened to him, but as the story of a friend of his from his youth. Moments later, Martha reveals that George had written a book about the incident which her father had suppressed. Further, she informs us that George had told her father that he was the young boy and that the novel was really an autobiography. Finally, the story is brought up again when George informs Martha of the telegram that supposedly had arrived informing them of the death of their son - he had died in exactly the same way as the boy's father had. What does all this mean? It has been suggested, of course, that George is actually the young boy and that this early tragic incident stunted his emotional growth and thus caused not only his failure but also his inability to assert his manhood. In such a view, he has become totally reliant on Martha for both her leadership in the family unit and for the punishment he feels he deserves. However, this is a tenuous reading of an extremely ambiguous string of connections. A far more plausible explanation, one which has already been mentioned, is that the young boy is also a fantasy child which George has conceived of and has since identified with. Nick lends credibility to such a view when, reacting to the incongruities between what George had told him and the story Martha tells, he says, "I don't know when you people are lying, or what."

Thus Albee presents a maze of lies and illusions, ambiguities which, although they confuse someone who is trying to work out all the details into a coherent whole, are meant to fully characterize the lives of George and Martha. For both of them have become so caught up in a world of fantasy that neither is able clearly to differentiate between truth and illusion and they are, in fact, headed on the same course to oblivion as that of Julian in *Tiny Alice*. It is very significant to note, however, that in "offering up" the imagined child for the purgation of the last scene, George connects it with his own story of the young boy and thus both are subjected to the exorcism and symbolic death rite: the cleansing action is thus a total one.

The fact that illusion permeates George and Martha's private universe is by now an obvious one; also, we have seen that although both are dependent on illusions, neither one has found happiness and both exist on the lowest level of emotional stability. The need for the action which George takes is clear, but what are his motives? What finally prompts him to take action in destroying the child? During the course of the evening, as the liquor and exhaustion strip him of his immunity and insulation from Martha's taunts, and as Martha's attacks grow in vehemence, George is finally pushed to take decisive action. As we have noted in our analysis of the action, as Martha's attacks increase in intensity, so do George's immediate emotional responses: tale about boxing/murder enactment with toy shotgun; story of his failures/smashing of bottle; revelation of the novel/attempted strangling; adultery (as he believes)/death of child. Thus the progression of the play and its rising intensity propels George to action and his immediate motive seems to be revenge: "I've got to figure out some new way to fight you." As Martha gradually exhausts herself, George's fury and his resolve increase to the point at which he initiates his great scheme. But even in the second act, "Walpurgisnacht", George's presence of mind seems to sharpen when he joins in Martha's games and becomes, in fact, the gamemaster in introducing the games against Nick and Honey and also Martha's "game" with Nick. In the final exorcistic action George is in full command, much to Martha's horror, and his drive to destroy the illusion is irreversible.

It would be inaccurate to conclude, however, that George's sole motive is revenge. Possibly it is in his initial motivating drive, but as we see at the end of the play, all animosity between them has vanished and his real purpose was to destroy the evils which caused her frenetic behavior rather than to hurt Martha herself. At the end of the play, George has normalized the household and freed both himself and Martha from the painful refuge of illusion.

NICK AND HONEY

Nick is the embodiment of the American Dream, a cultural phenomenon which has occupied Albee in the past. He represents and indeed epitomizes a number of characteristics which, in Albee's view, Americans regard as sure ingredients of success: a perfectly balanced combination of intelligence, extremely handsome features, a powerfully athletic physique, a naive enthusiasm and belief in the future, and a showcase wife. Thus Nick is ostensibly perfect and can boast all the commercial attributes of success. Moreover, he has risen quickly through the ranks of undergraduate and graduate school to become an unusually precocious and talented biology instructor and, of course, his plans for rising much higher in the ranks are already laid out. Nick is coldly calculating, ambitious, and, to say the least, opportunistic. Indeed, he considers it advantageous to become a favorite with the daughter of the college president and thus cooperates in Martha's drive to humiliate George.

In the course of the play both Nick and Honey come under Albee's close scrutiny and their marriage is revealed to be far from the ideal image which Nick wishes to project. In the second conversation with George, as we saw in the summary of the action, he makes two highly significant revelations: he married Honey because she thought she was pregnant, and Honey had inherited a good sum of money from her father, a religious fraud-thus a potentially unpleasant situation for Nick has neutralized itself because he can use the money to further his career. Nevertheless, their marriage is grounded on illusion and therefore potentially destructive. The implication is present that twenty years from now they will be quite as miserable as George and Martha are today.

George's revulsion at the young man is quite understandable since Nick's aggressiveness is exactly what George lacks and he recognizes in him precisely the kind of husband Martha had once envisioned. Certainly Nick would be willing to be groomed to assume the presidency of the college, a goal which he probably holds at the present moment. However, the differences between the two men go far deeper than that: Nick and George are also representatives of two opposing cultures - science and humanism. Nick demonstrates an unbounded confidence in the future and in the ability of science to produce a race of miracle-men through genetic selection. He is the "wave of the future" who will rise to dominate other men -a "small **irony**" was intended in invoking the association of Nick's name with that of Nikita Khrushchev who was then in power. George, on the other hand, has spent far too long studying the past and in studying his own marriage to accept any of Nick's optimism. Despite his cynicism, George is still a humanist who realizes the fallacy of Nick's naive and potentially dangerous position. It is also apparent that Nick's faith in the future is but one way a person can avoid unpleasant reality; in his case it is his marriage.

Quite ironically, the effect of the evening's steady drinking has opposite effects on the two men - as George is pushed into taking action and finally assumes the male role of the household, Nick's aura of perfection begins to disintegrate. The glaring evidence of this is, of course, his impotence in the final drive Martha mounts to hurt George - even the American Dream cannot withstand the deadening effects of alcohol and exhaustion. After this incident Martha viciously puts Nick down, relegating him to the role of houseboy and openly accusing him of opportunistic motives.

Albee has been criticized for his characterization of Nick, specifically in that the revelation Nick makes about his marriage in the second act is unprepared for up to that point and is therefore inconsistent. Such a criticism seems justified because Nick is far too superficial and noncommittal a person to purposely, without any apparent reason, break his facade of perfection in admitting such a human "accident." Also, the revelation itself is very significant, since it serves to place the two marriages on the same level, and thus it should have been better prepared for. Instead, Albee has devoted the greater part of his attention to the portrayal of George and Martha. It was a problem to manipulate both male roles to accommodate all the major plot elements that Albee wanted to include.

Honey is the most comic of the characters, the most thinly drawn and in some ways meant to be the most deceptive. In appearance she is a plain, petite blond of twenty-six who tends to substitute a non-committal giggle for intelligent comment and who has a bad habit of sucking her thumb. Martha describes her with characteristic candor as being "a mousy little type" who lacks "hips," etc. But despite her intellectual shallowness, Honey is a rather suitable mate for the American Dream - she is pleasant and makes a presentable appearance, she can deliver generous praise and cliched compliments when the moment demands, as she does upon their arrival at George and Martha's home. More importantly, however, she is not nearly intelligent enough to ever compete with Nick on either an intellectual or social level. Honey is a rather pathetic figure throughout the play, as well as a comic one - she is quite unaware that Nick and Martha are carrying on and certainly does not realize the significance of what occurs in the exorcism ritual, although she is frightened by its intensity. Honey spends most of the evening "sipping" brandy and becomes increasingly inebriated and thus provides some needed humor in her periodic periods of nausea which occur at moments of particular stress in George and Martha's battle.

In addition Nick's revelation about her hysterical pregnancy, which George publicizes to the entire company, we learn that Honey now has a fear of childbearing, which adds an additional liability to the future of their marriage. Thus the two couples are compared and contrasted and found to be quite alike despite Nick and Honey's youth-Albee shows us a marriage which contains all of the potentially self-destructive elements which have soured George and Martha's. The purgation action, therefore, is aimed at all four people and the hope is raised that each one will benefit in their own way.

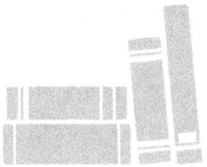

WHO'S AFRAID OF VIRGINIA WOOLF?

THE MEANING OF WHO'S AFRAID OF VIRGINIA WOOLF?

IMPORTANT QUESTIONS ABOUT THE MEANING

What are the major **themes** of the play? What is the function and meaning of the imaginary child? What does Albee say in the play about the nature of illusion and how does he say it? What is significant about the title of the play? What are the play's political themes? Why have some critics suggested that the play could aptly be retitled Long Night's Journey Into Day? The following discussion will attempt to arrive at some answers to these questions. There are many elements in the play which are ambiguous and do not lend themselves to being fitted into a comprehensive interpretation. What is most clear, however, it that there is a strong continuity of **theme** between this major work and the rest of Albee's plays.

Who's Afraid of Virginia Woolf? has several important characteristics in common with Albee's earlier play, *The Death of Bessie Smith*, which can be used as starting point in considering major themes. Although the basic focus in the present play is the relationship of members in the family unit, the bases of conflict and the tone of both plays are very similar. Both depict naturalistic conflicts which contain a marked element of exaggeration reaching to the very edge of absurdity. Like those in *The Death of Bessie Smith*, the characters of *Who's Afraid of Virginia Woolf?* are trapped in a closed, static universe. Though there are highly destructive elements inherent in each of these universes which torment the inhabitants, they are dependent on these same elements for their ability to function in society. The emotional crescendos reached by the Intern and Nurse have a common origin with those of George and Martha: frustration of hopes and the inability to obtain either sexual or spiritual fulfillment, the dependence on and simultaneous loathing of the world in which they live-a world which is isolated from reality. The only kind of human contact either couple is capable of is their abusive insults which substitute for both ordinary communication and even for sexual union. There are also illusions: Intern and Nurse speak of the pleasurable consummation of their mutual attraction to each other and both dream of breaking away from the depressed South to a better life. Even the black Orderly has the illusion of fitting into white society and disassociating himself from his race. Martha, of course, has the child and George has the young boy and his study of the past. Finally, what emerges in both plays is an existential grief, a feeling of nausea, at the state of their existence.

The major **theme** of *Who's Afraid of Virginia Woolf?*, then, is the failure of man to face reality and to deal with it without being overwhelmed and destroyed. Instead, man resorts to illusion in order to avoid the pain and invariable disappointment inherent in facing reality. In the case of George and Martha, they live in a world which revolves around a central illusion, the imaginary child, which is complete with a detailed mythology formed slowly over the years. Such a mythic creation lends meaning to their lives and enables them to express affection and to give of their love without having to give it to each other-in fact, they find their partners unworthy of love. In the sense of these many evasions and hostilities, their marriage resembles millions of others in a society in which there is a total transference of mutual affection to a "third party" - a child, perhaps, or even to animals or material objects. It is a way of avoiding communication and recognition of failures and imperfections. George and Martha have been called Mr. and Mrs. America, not because of their social status which is culturally elitist, but because their marriage is so very familiar.

It is quite apparent that Albee is not primarily concerned with the original shortcomings in either George or Martha which prompted them to find refuge in illusion. The major causal factor is supplied, but there is no reason to assume that there were not others - perhaps very slight, insignificant ones. But what is certain is that none of the reasons we are informed of are at all extraordinary - they are simply human inadequacies. The specific example of George's failure to become president of the college is, in principle, like any other failure of more common goals.

The presence and participation of Nick and Honey in the games George and Martha play enables Albee to broaden the thematic implications of the play. They are important for two reasons: First, the state of their marriage is closely parallel to that of George and Martha's. They were married under the supposition that Honey was pregnant and thus the haunting question will always remain: Would the American Dream have married the "Blondie-type" girl without this added impetus? And since their marriage Honey has developed a fear of pregnancy which puts a further strain on the stability of their marriage.

The second factor is that Nick possesses a simplistic definition and formula for success. George's deep cynicism, which is grounded in many truthful insights into history, is contrasted with Nick's undaunted confidence in the future and in the potentialities of science. Nick is the modern-day Faust, the "wave of the future" who would replace the arts with science, feeling with cold practicality, and liberty with genetic legislation. But Nick's philosophy is seen for what it is by Martha who tells him: "You see everything but the god damned mind."

Albee also takes to task George's dependence on a study of the past to judge the present. His so-called "wisdom" has given him nothing more than the brooding realization, a useless one, that the entire world is little different from the state of his marriage. What he can do is recognize, but not correct, the fallacies of both outlooks. He recognizes that both are illusions:

When people can't abide ... the present ... either they turn to a contemplation of the past, ... or they set about to ... alter the future!

Thus Albee makes it clear that his play concerns both the very intimate kinds of illusions which people create as well as the public ones originated and sustained on a much broader scale; they are equally as deceptive and potentially as destructive. In *Who's Afraid of Virginia Woolf?* the two worlds meet. Albee develops the related **theme** that where illusion lives, there is also inherent decay, corruption, waste. Although George's cynicism is at times overpowering, he is perhaps not off-base in comparing his marriage with Western civilization, especially at the moment when it appears that Martha and Nick are committing adultery.

To emphasize the pervasiveness of illusion and decay, Albee inserts several powerful allusions: The name of the town and college in which George teaches, for example, is New Carthage - an **allusion** to the ancient city of Carthage which was founded by the Phoenicians and centuries later totally destroyed by the Romans who leveled it and strewed the ground with salt to make the earth permanently sterile. The history of its phenomenal prosperity and decadence has become a symbol throughout literature of sterility and false values. Perhaps the most famous use of the **allusion** is, significantly, in T.S. Eliot's poem "The Waste Land". He uses it here to characterize the modern age and in the notes to the poem he quotes St. Augustine's *Confessions* in which the ancient bishop comments on the evil of the city: "To Carthage then I came, where a cauldron of unholy loves sang all about mine ears!" A number of other cities with relevant **connotations** are also added: George compares New Carthage with Ilyria, the seacoast setting of Shakespeare's *Twelfth Night* - it is a place of love madness in which there is a reversal of sexes by clothing disguise and an eventual return to normal sexual identities and a happy ending for all; and with Penguin Island, Anatole France's mythic island which the inhabitants were overcome and ultimately destroyed by capitalism; finally, with Gomorrah, the infamous Biblical city destroyed by God as a punishment for its corruption.

The message of the play, then, applies to more than just the family unit and carries a strong political **theme**, although it is less explicitly stated than in *The Death of Bessie Smith*. The merging of private and public illusions and the destructive quality which is seen therefore in both, makes it clear that Albee's intended view is a broad expanse beginning with an individual and his intimate family relationships and proceeding outward through levels of society to finally encompassing all of civilization. Illusion and decay are pervasive malignities which make their effects known wherever and whenever men are forced to confront reality and are overpowered by its prospect.

TITLE OF THE PLAY

Albee first intended the title of this play to be *The Exorcism*, but then changed it when he saw the phrase "Who's Afraid of Virginia Woolf?" written on a graffiti wall in a Greenwich Village bar. It is intended to mean: "Who is afraid of facing life without illusions?" The **refrain** is sung several times in the play, first as a joke which the drunken hosts and their hosts and their guests find hilarious. However, it gradually assumes a far more serious meaning when at the end of the second act George sings it as Martha comes to the **climax** of her recitation of his failure. In this context he means it as a threat - an early indication of the consequence she faces in attempting to humiliate him. Finally in the final moments of the play, the **rhyme** becomes a tender question which really needs no answer - Martha is certainly afraid of what life without her precious illusion will hold. The phrase, which at first seems an incongruous title for a play of cruelty and abuse, becomes understood as an important leitmotif in tracing the progression of the action.

CONCLUSION

The destruction of the imaginary child in the ritualistic exorcism frees the characters from their illusions and breaks the fury and sterility of the game world in which combat replaced communication. All of the characters have had their failures and illusions "offered up" and symbolically destroyed. George has demonstrated the ability and necessity of man to directly attack the "evils" which infect his life and to radically re-order his existence - "accommodation, malleability, adjustment" in the face of reality has given way to direct, assertive action. George and Martha are left at the door, exhausted, with the prospect of having to face a frightening and uncertain future without the comfort of their illusions. But although it is very uncertain that they will find happiness, Albee rejects the tragic determinism of O'Neill and the Absurdists; rather, he gives his characters a "fighting chance" to make their own way in the world and find fulfillment. George and Martha will now have to accept each other and their mutual imperfections, and Nick will hopefully temper his Faustian zeal with a more sensitive and moral humanism. Perhaps Nick and Honey will come to establish a really solid marriage and Honey will accept the reality of her sexuality.

But how does the resolution apply to the broader social and political implications of the play? First of all, we have already emphasized the fact that the opposing outlooks or philosophies of Nick and George are purposely tied to the private illusions and deceits of the couples' marriages; therefore, the purgative action of the final act is aimed at all these elements. Both the public and private illusions have been characterized as fallacious and potentially destructive and thus Albee is concerned not only with the survival of individuals and family units, but also with society in general. Secondly, the play has been termed a "political allegory" - it is an allegory in the sense that Albee is as much criticizing a general way of life as he is a specific relationship. His conviction about the danger of constantly seeking escape from reality is applicable on all levels of society. In the very recognizable setting of *Who's Afraid of Virginia Woolf?*, however, Albee utilizes his favorite **theme** of the desecration and decay of the family unit to depict this harmful approach to existence. It is in this specific sense that the actions of George and Martha can be seen as possible paradigms of actions on other levels of society, all of which have the same end -escape from reality. But it is important to realize that the play is not a true allegory in the sense that characters are strictly types or personifications. George and Martha are real people with realistic shortcomings and fears and the terror they feel in dealing with reality is a very human one. Although Nick and Honey are thinly drawn, their presence is functional rather than allegorical. In sum, Albee leads us to draw many broad implications from his work, but all of them are meant to come from within the framework of the actions of his characters.

ALBEE AND O'NEILL

In rejecting illusion as a basis for existence and the theater as a means of escape, Albee's position is directly contrasted with that of Eugene O'Neill. O'Neill also loathed illusion and recognized it as a serious type of untruth, but was also all-too-aware of the pain and tragedy inherent in reality. His characters are extremely human creations complete with painful failures and they find existence possible only with the security of illusion - most typically in the past when there was fleeting happiness. Who can forget the haunting sight of Larry in the final scene of *The Iceman Cometh* as he sits at the window, staring blankly at a brick wall and thus depicting what man is reduced to when he cannot arm himself with illusion. In *The Iceman Cometh* the character Hickey sets himself to be a savior who seeks to raise his friends out of their many kinds of escapes from reality - "pipedreams," alcohol, reminiscences of the past, etc. He finds, however, that his efforts have not brought his friends happiness, but only false hopes and then an even deeper reversion to illusion in order to avoid this latest failure. As Larry says, "Can't you see there is no tomorrow now?"

In *Long Day's Journey Into Night*, perhaps O'Neill's greatest play, he examines the history of sickness and failure of the

Tyrone family and traces their journey away from reality. The world, they discover, is a place of pain and disappointment; they come to a terrible conclusion about man: "We are such stuff as manure is made on." One can recognize a strong bond between the characters of O'Neill's plays and those of Albee's since both men recognize the world's hostility and uncertainty; however, O'Neill is far too merciful and has himself suffered too much pain to destroy his characters' illusions. Rather, he presents them for what they are - evasions and lies, but still allows them to remain. One type of illusion which O'Neill uses most often is that of the past where, as one character says, "truth is untrue and life can hide from itself." Thus the title of his play *Long Day's Journey Into Night* describes a passage into the throes of illusion - no solution is offered, no reality is changed.

It has been suggested that Albee's play could aptly be renamed Long Night's Journey Into Day since what occurs is a rite of passage out of illusion into an uncertain and dangerous reality. George and Martha are freed of their great illusions and must now take their chances depending on each other which, as we have noted, is the most optimistic note of salvation that Albee can sound.

GAME-PLAY AND RITUAL IN WHO'S AFRAID OF VIRGINIA WOOLF?

Although the basic conflict of the play is the naturalistic battle of the sexes, *Who's Afraid of Virginia Woolf?* appreciably transcends Strindberg's theater through the use of game-play and ritual as its central structural components. Some critics have felt that this was a needless distortion, but few could deny that they are major contributive factors to the effectiveness of the play. One reason for seeking to transcend orthodox naturalism is, of course, to serve the interests of originality, which is what Albee has accomplished. In the process, however, he has drawn upon both Strindberg's battle of the sexes and Genet's Theater of Cruelty to construct a powerful drama and to make a major statement about man's survival in the modern world. Game-play and ritual, major techniques in Theater of Cruelty, are integral elements in the confrontation with reality which Albee forces on both his characters and the audience. Specifically, they perform several major functions in the play:

First, the game and ritual structure of the play emphasizes the all-important fact that the world of George and Martha is far removed from reality. The illusion of the child is the **metaphysical** center of their private universe, the boundaries of which are their household. It is so expressedly private and withdrawn that rules of society do not apply within its precincts and the participants in the games establish their own rules-the major one is that the illusionary child is not to be mentioned to anyone outside the game circle. When this central rule is breached, some kind of punitive action is called for, thus forming a less obvious (and less important) pretext for the action which George takes. In effect, the imposition of a game structure sets up isolating boundaries and produces recognizable order on that private world in which rampant hostility could easily result in emotional chaos. Through this order these emotions are shaped into individual units constituting the illusion-centered world and their value in portraying the tormented existences of George and Martha is maximized.

A second function is that the game structure establishes a vortex movement which leads the characters and the audience progressively deeper into the structure of the two marriages and reveals the many shortcomings and failures which pervade each of them. The "fun and games" of the first act are primarily unstructured, but as the play unfolds, they take on a more formal effect, even to the extent of having a gamemaster announce them, give them names and direct them. This growth in seriousness and intensity is indicative of the deepening penetration which is being made into the emotional cores of the characters. Such obvious violations of a naturalistic structure, however, do not mitigate the bitterness or tremendous destructive power of Martha and George's battles and their attacks on Nick and Honey; if anything, the impact is increased, since it is confined in the boundaries of the game and is therefore made more prominent. Thus Albee willingly accepts exaggeration for the sake of heightened emotion, dramatic effectiveness, and a clearer definition of his intentions. This is what he has called the creation of a "selective reality" in which conflicts and shortcomings are taken directly from life and in the dramatic process are made more effective through some degree of "selection and hyperbole." However, neither the basic nature nor the inherent evil of either marriage is distorted-it is actually brought into clearer relief.

Third, the game-play and ritual of the play demonstrates Albee's awareness of man's basic nature. Along with cruelty and violence, game and ritual formed the basis of the earliest drama-the Dionysian sacrificial rituals. Thus Albee, because he deals with both very private as well as public illusions, seeks to penetrate layers of civilization and achieve his effect on a very fundamental basis of man's understanding. Game-play has been recognized as being at the heart of many aspects of man's behavior in everyday life-both Johan Huizinga's Homo Ludens and Eric Berne's Games People Play seek to demonstrate this fact. From having reviewed the action of the play it is apparent that *Who's Afraid of Virginia Woolf?* closely follows Huizinga's summary of major game elements: "order, tension, movement, change, solemnity, rhythm, rapture." The games of the play create total involvement and thus provide the basis for the cathartic resolution at the end.

The ritual of the long final scene is perhaps, one of the most painful moments of theater seen in recent times. Its tremendous dramatic power is aimed at destroying the many evils which have become visible and, most of all, the illusion of the child-it is a powerful statement by the dramatist of his feelings toward illusions: they must be deliberately, systematically and even quite "religiously" destroyed. The fact that the ritual is both an Exorcism (which was to be the original title of the play) and a Requiem indicates, as we have noted, that illusion is both a curse to man and one of his pathetically precious possessions. Albee makes use of the Latin rites of the ancient Christian Church to stress the profound nature of what he is saying, and perhaps he felt that a naturalistic statement would be adequate.

In this play, as well as in *The Zoo Story* and *Tiny Alice*, there are either actual or symbolic death scenes which arouse a great deal of emotion. This and his usage of cruelty and violence makes Albee's theater akin to Genet's wild theater of bizarre spectacle, games, wish-fulfillment fantasies and rituals. Both playwrights recognize that all of these elements appeal to man's deepest sensibilities. Although Genet de-emphasizes language in favor of spectacle, both seek a full **exposition** of the evils which afflict man. What Sartre wrote of Genet seems to apply closely to *Who's Afraid of Virginia Woolf?*, as well as to many of Albee's other plays: "By affecting us with his evil, Genet delivers us from it." Thus like Genet's Theater of Cruelty, Albee's Theater of Confrontation attempts to penetrate man's inner core of emotion and communicate with him on the most intimate of levels. Albee has taken care to construct a dramatic form using game and ritual which has the power to destroy illusion, since man will never give it up willingly.

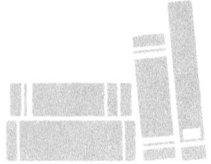

WHO'S AFRAID OF VIRGINIA WOOLF?

ESSAY QUESTIONS AND ANSWERS

Question: What is the function of game-play and ritual in *Who's Afraid of Virginia Woolf?* How successful are these techniques?

Answer: The entire action of the play, with the exception of the final scene, consists of a series of game units which vary in intensity and formal demarcation, i.e., they begin as rapidly moving verbal confrontations between George and Martha, George and Nick, etc., and proceed to the formal, more deliberate games of the "Walpurgisnacht." The overall result, of course, is that the characters are made to face the reality of their lives. One major result of both game-play and ritual is the powerful dramatic effectiveness which is achieved. There is a building up of tension as the games increase in intensity and deadly-earnest cruelty becomes the ruling passion of the participants in the games. Audiences who have viewed either the stage production of the work or the motion picture version have found the play extremely effective and, indeed, both painful and fatiguing to watch. Some critics have favorably compared its dramatic effectiveness with that of O'Neill's *Long Day's Journey Into Night*, a play which sets out to accomplish much the same tasks, but which reaches diverse conclusions. Certainly the most serious, climactic game of the play, the formal "Exorcism," is a purely electric moment of tension and perhaps even of agony as the audience witnesses the most painful of all the confrontations of the play: the realization that Martha's precious son is an illusion and that it is being willfully and systematically destroyed and, further, that she is an unwilling yet helpless partner in that destruction. Despite Diana Trilling's critical explanation for the play's effect, *Who's Afraid of Virginia Woolf?* does succeed, through its game and ritual structure, to deeply involve an audience in an examination of the illusions on which so many people depend for their existences. To achieve this effect there is an obvious transcendence of strict naturalism, yet a faithful portrayal of the sterile emptiness of the illusion-ridden spirit.

This latter point must be considered a second major function of the games and ritual: to create what Albee calls a "selective reality" which focuses attention on specific aspects of reality of the human condition. We are given crystallized, precise insights into the marriages of both couples and into the numerous yet closely related "evils" which are undermining their very existences and, in the case of George and Martha, which make their lives a literal "hell on earth." The stylized demarcations of the formal games and final elaborate ritual are best appreciated when one takes heed of Albee's long-standing advice, which he feels is applicable to all his plays: to allow the action and the message of the play to act upon the unconscious in a kind of composite implosion. It is in the final realization which is achieved in the minds of the viewers that Albee's play conveys the greatest truths.

Anthony Hilfer (and others as well) feels that the ritual **climax** of the play and the entire conception of the illusory child are quite unbelievable and little more than sheer theatrical devices. The ritual especially, in Helfer's view, is "out of context" and is a serious detriment to the integrity of the play. He points out that the sudden stylization of a Latin rite is hardly consistent with what has taken place in the previous two and a half acts. There are, however, several cogent factors which make such usage understandable and quite consistent with what preceded it. First, the Catholic ritual called "Exorcism" has its roots in the earliest of ancient religious cults and is thus at the very basis of Western civilization; it appeals not simply to precise religious beliefs of a certain religion, but to the basic response of man to the frightening and mystifying world in which he lives. Like the game-play, the ritual of *Who's Afraid of Virginia Woolf?* attempts to involve modern man in a deeply moving dramatic experience and like *The Zoo Story* and *Tiny Alice*, seeks to stimulate the most elemental and consequently the most profound of responses. Second, it has been noted that the essentially conflicting aspects of the ritual (Requiem and Exorcism) delineate the nature of illusion as it affects man. It is this disparity which accounts for so much of the torment we see in Martha; she is totally committed to the sustenance of the illusion yet loathing it for the misery it wreaks on both her and George. Thus in being aware that the ritual follows a tightly controlled intensification of a game structure and also reflects the playwright's conceptualization of the central **theme**, one can hardly conclude that the ritual is inappropriate. Perhaps what is at the core of Albee's rather "spectacular" drama is an understanding much like Genet's of what is most potent in appealing to man's fundamental nature.

Question: In what ways does *Who's Afraid of Virginia Woolf?* achieve thematic transcendence?

Answer: It is entirely consistent with what we have seen as Albee's abiding social commitment that he should attempt to make this play descriptive not only of a specific situation in life, but also that he seek to make a statement of much broader import. A careful reading of the play offers rather generous indications of the playwright's intended statement. The most fundamental observation which can be made, of course, is that Albee has presented yet another in-depth study of the marital unit - the fundamental social grouping on which our society is built. With this core situation it becomes apparent that Albee is concerned not only with George and Martha's specific tortures, but with the quality of their existence in general - their hateful behavior to each other and the kinds of things they use to instill meaning in their lives are by no means peculiar to them, but they are meant to reflect millions of couples who have lost sight of their mutual love and who have ceased communicating and touching. George indicates with a sweep of his hand that neither the deceitful occurrences nor animosities which infect his home or even the community of New Carthage are so terribly uncommon; in fact, such things as illusion, corruption of morals, and sheer waste are historical constants and will most likely continue to exist. It is this broad realization of the serious inadequacies and utter failing of society and his consistent attacks on those imperfections that connects Albee so closely with the literature of the "Waste Land". Thus the illusion, corruption, jealousy, greed, and cruelty - and the suffering and ultimate destruction they cause - are universal elements and like the specific locale of the action, Albee's powerful statement expressed in the final ritual scene is equally as universal.

Another more literal transcendence which is expressed in the play and which has already been emphasized, is the explicit political **theme** embodied in the conflict between the two conflicting cultures represented by George and Nick. Their respective philosophies or world outlooks are the public kinds of illusion - those which an entire nation or even a society adopts as one of its principal ethics. And Albee makes it clear that the illusions of an unbalanced faith in both the past and the future are equally as dangerous, especially in the present nuclear age. Thus with the specific thematic strains of the horrific marital relationship and the world outlooks, Albee develops a broad-based statement about the way in which men live and tragically waste their lives, and the destructiveness of illusion as a means of avoiding those realities.

Despite the fact that the play lends itself to allegorical interpretations and that the characters can conceivably be identified as types, it must be emphasized that this is not the playwright's intent - Albee is dealing with human beings and the suffering and abuse which we witness in the play are totally human. Albee concentrates on a specific societal unit, but makes it clear that the quality of the existence he portrays and the basic approach to reality through illusion are quite as applicable to any social plane.

Serious questions have been raised, however, as to whether or not the central symbol of the illusory child is handled properly in conveying this thematic implication; specifically, Anthony Hilfer has claimed that the "slaughtering" of the child in the ritual event has been inadequately prepared for. This criticism does seem to have some validity; however, it is not a fatal flaw that clouds the author's intentions. The chief consequence of the child's confusing and totally enigmatic "presence" in Acts I and II is that the third act becomes the most crucial one in terms of resolving the central symbol of the child.

Question: What is the place of this play in the contemporary theater?

Answer: Despite a number of persistent criticisms which have been leveled against *Who's Afraid of Virginia Woolf?* - its length, heavy-handed and unclear symbolism, and echoes of other writers, etc. - the play is generally regarded as Albee's all-around best work. It solidly established Albee as America's leading new playwright and some critics even ventured to speculate that Albee could conceivably achieve the stature of O'Neill if he continued to grow with such great artistry. This prognosis seemed especially relevant since the "greats" of the fifties' decade, Arthur Miller and Tennessee Williams, seemed to be sliding rapidly from the forefront of American theater. Albee's subsequent works, however, have been met with rather subdued and often extremely hostile criticism; but much of this adverse reaction has been incredibly narrow-minded and at times quite unwarranted. Perhaps the clearest judgment that we can offer of plays which followed *Who's Afraid of Virginia Woolf?* is that it is quite possible that Albee has sacrificed polished artistry in the vein of this play for the sake of continued experimentation and dramaturgical innovation. Albee has obviously traveled a great distance in technique from his initial plays such as *The American Dream*; his latest play, *All Over*, might well prove to be the start of another great period of artistic development utilizing the characteristics of musical form and challenging the audience to abandon its conventional expectations of what a drama should be.

Aside from its position as the most famous and best play by an American dramatist of the sixties, *Who's Afraid of Virginia Woolf?* is also important for the conception of man which it demonstrates. Albee's view of man represents an important departure from the ruling Absurdists of the post-war era - it centers around a sustained belief in the ability of man to act and to maintain his human dignity in the face of an ever-increasing reality of sufferings and uncertainty. While Absurdist Theater focuses on visibly decaying, desperate creatures, Albee presents us with human situations in which there is misery and great suffering, and he resolves such situations with rather simple, truly unheroic victories for man. Jerry, George, Tobias - all demonstrate a severely damaged, even crushed humanity, yet all retain the ability to act when a crisis develops. It is in presenting such a clear enactment of this philosophic conception that *Who's Afraid of Virginia Woolf?* is so important as a departure from the Absurd. Albee seeks to confront both his characters and the audience with the realities of their existence, with the inadequacies and corruption which pervade their lives and the society in which they live; Albee talks about wasted lives, wasted time. This play is a succinct crystallization of this view and its undeniable affirmation at the final tableau is perhaps one of the most significant and, indeed, beautiful moments of theater in recent times. What emerges is both a faith in man and an impassioned and even desperate call for a revival of love and honesty, of simple human communication in the face of terrifying reality.

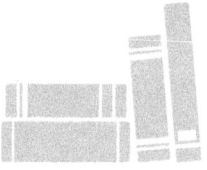

BIBLIOGRAPHY

WORKS OF EDWARD ALBEE

(Those marked by asterisks are in popularly-priced paperback editions.)

All Over. New York: Atheneum, 1971.

The American Dream and *The Zoo Story*.^* New York: Signet Book (New American Library), 1963.

The Ballad of the Sad Café. Boston: Houghton Mifflin, 1963.

Box and *Quotations from Chairman Mao Tse-Tung*.^* New York: Signet Books, 1970.

A Delicate Balance.^* New York: Pocket Books, 1966.

Everything in the Garden.^* New York: Pocket Books, 1969.

Malcolm, New York: Atheneum, 1966.

The Sandbox and *The Death of Bessie Smith*.^* New York: Signet Books, 1966. (Also contains *Fam and Yam*.)

Tiny Alice.^* New York: Pocket Books, 1965.

Who's Afraid of Virginia Woolf?.^* New York: Pocket Books, 1963.

OTHER WORKS

"Apartheid in the Theater." *New York Times*, July 30, 1967, II, pp. 1, 6.

"Novel Beginning," *Esquire*, LX (July 1963), pp. 59-60.

"Introduction." *Three Plays by Noel Coward*. New York: Dell Publishing Company, 1965.

"Which Theater is the Absurd One?" *New York Times Magazine*, (February 25, 1962), 30-31, 64, 66. Reprinted in *American Playwrights on Drama*, edited by Horst Frenz. New York: Hill and Wang, 1965, 168-74; and in John Gassner's *Directions in Modern Theater and Drama*. New York: Holt, Rinehart and Winston, 1965.

"Who's Afraid of the Truth?" *New York Times*, Sunday drama section (August 18, 1963), 1.

"Who Is James Purdy?" *New York Times*, Sunday drama section (January 9, 1966), 1, 3.

"The Writer as Independent Spirit: 6. Creativity and Commitment." *Saturday Review*, XLIX (June 4, 1966), 26.

INTERVIEWS

Diehl, Digby. "Edward Albee Interviewed." *Transatlantic Review*, XIII (Summer 1963), 57-72.

Flanagan, William. "The Art of the Theater IV. Edward Albee." *The Paris Review*, XXXIX (Fall 1966), 92-121.

Stewart, R. S. "John Gielgud and Edward Albee Talk about the Theater." *Atlantic* CCXV (April 1965), 61-8.

Rutenberg, Michael E. "Two Interviews with Edward Albee." *Edward Albee: Playwright in Protest*. New York: DBS Publications, Inc., 1969, 229-60.

"What's It About? - A Playwright Tries to Tell." *New York Herald Tribune Magazine*, "The Lively Arts" (January 22, 1961), 5.

CRITICAL STUDIES

The following is by no means an exhaustive bibliography. We have attempted to cull the most valuable studies and those which might prove most relevant toward a further study of the plays.)

Amacher, Richard E. *Edward Albee*. New York: Twayne Publishers, Inc., 1969. A useful introduction to Albee's work ending with *A Delicate Balance*. Essays dealing with the various plays provide insightful analyses of intricate actions and dialogues, but many judgments which are given are rather dubious and should always be balanced with other studies.

Baxandall, Lee. "The Theatre of Edward Albee." *Tulane Drama Review*, 9 (1965), 19-40. One of the first long studies of the early plays; stresses Albee's concern with the foils and foibles of the institution of the American family.

Bigsby, C. W. *E. Albee*. Edinburgh, Scotland: Oliver and Boyd; Ltd., 1969. Probably the most well-balanced, thoughtful and readable study of Albee's career up to *A Delicate Balance*. Contains one of the few discussions of Albee's first writing published in the *Choate Literary Magazine*. It is Bigsby who first saw that Albee's drama differs importantly from that of the so-called existential rebels. He originated the term "Theater of Confrontation" in order to express this important differentiation.

Brustein, Robert. *The Theater of Revolt: An Approach to Modern Drama*. Boston: Little, Brown and Company, 1964. A fine survey of the major figures of modern drama beginning with Ibsen and Strindberg and concluding with an especially informative essay on Artaud and Genet. Albee is mentioned only in passing, and is identified with the existential revolt. Good background for study of Albee.

Coleman, D. C. "Fun and Games: Two Pictures of Heartbreak House." *Drama Survey*, 5 (Winter, 1966-67), 223-36. One of several interesting studies which attempt to identify sources and parallels with *Who's Afraid of Virginia Woolf?* This essay compares the characterization, setting, action and **themes** of Albee's play with Bernard Shaw's *Heartbreak House*. Takes note of the affirmative conclusion which Albee reaches and contrasts it with Shaw's pessimistic conclusion about the degenerated state of his own age.

Debusscher, Gilbert. *Edward Albee: Tradition and Renewal*. Translated by Anne W. Williams. Brussels: Center for American Studies, 1967. This is an interesting study ending with a consideration of *Tiny Alice*. Debusscher begins with a brief survey of American drama and notes the virtual hiatus in high dramatic quality which came after the gradual decline of Miller and Williams in the fifties; he finds Albee taking up the tradition of quality and social consciousness initiated by O'Neill. Thus his central thesis, which is summarized in the final chapter entitled "Albee: Tradition and Renewal", is that Albee is "the first to integrate the discoveries of the French avantgarde theater" and the first to synthesize this "new theater and the great American tradition derived from Ibsen and Strindberg."

Dozier, Richard J. "Adultery and Disappointment in *Who's Afraid of Virginia Woolf?*" *Modern Drama*, 11 (1968), 432-36. Objects to the abrupt change between the second and third acts; feels the audience should be allowed to draw its own conclusions from the games.

Driver, Tom F. *Romantic Quest and Modern Query: A History of the Modern Theater.* New York: Delacorte Press, Inc., 1970. Dismisses Albee as little more than a "culture hero" whose work suffers from both unoriginality and the constant attention paid to popular taste. Mr. Driver has consistently given Albee's plays unfavorable reviews: this study devotes less than a page to Albee. Driver's criticism is essentially unproved.

Dukore, Bernard F. "A Warp in Albee's Woolf." *Southern Speech Journal,* 30 (Spring 1965), 261-68. Points out parallels between the story elements and **imagery** of *Who's Afraid of Virginia Woolf?* and Euripides' *Medea.*

Esslin, Martin. *The Theater of the Absurd.* Garden City, New York: Doubleday and Company, Inc., revised edition, 1969. Famous and probably the best treatment of Absurdist drama. Albee is mentioned briefly and is grouped with young Absurdist playwrights.

Flasch, Mrs. Harold A. "Games People Play in *Who's Afraid of Virginia Woolf?*" *Modern Drama,* 10 (December 1967), 280-88. Applies the major principles of Eric Berne's *Games People Play* to Albee's work.

Harris, Wendell V. "Morality, Absurdity and Albee." *Southwest Review,* 49 (1964), 249-56. Views the plays up to *Who's Afraid of Virginia Woolf?* as black, absurd attacks on American society, but finds the first real note of affirmation in George's action and the final tableau.

Hilfer, Anthony C. "George and Martha: Sad, Sad, Sad," in *Seven Contemporary Authors,* Thomas B. Whitbread, ed. Austin: University of Texas Press, 1966, 119-39. Offers some interesting criticisms of *Who's Afraid of Virginia Woolf?*

Lewis, Allen. "The Fun and Games of Edward Albee." *Educational Theater Journal*, 16 (1964), 29-39. An informative general discussion of the plays, concentrating on *Who's Afraid of Virginia Woolf?* Feels the play demonstrates a relationship with the work of Beckett and Strindberg.

Macdonald, Daniel. "Truth and Illusion in *Who's Afraid of Virginia Woolf?*" *Renascence*, 17 (1964), 63-69. Offers the thesis that Albee's play demonstrates the "necessity of illusion," but this has been often contested and such a view is now primarily a minority one.

Meyer, Ruth. "Language: Truth and Illusion in *Who's Afraid of Virginia Woolf?*" *Educational Theater Journal*, 20 (1968), 60-69. An excellent analysis of the language of ambiguity and contradiction in which all the characters in the play participate in order to protect their true natures.

Nelson, Gerald. "Edward Albee and his Well-Made Plays." *Tri-Quarterly*, 5 (n.d.), 182-88. Offers the view that Albee ruins his own work by constantly sacrificing powerful drama for the sake of explication.

Oberg, A. K. "Edward Albee: His Language and Imagination." *Prairie Schooner*, 40 (Summer, 1966), 139-46. A fine essay on the elements of Albee's powerful language.

Otten, Terry. "Ibsen and Albee's Spurious Children." *Comparative Drama*, 2 (Spring 1968), 83-93. Finds close parallels between *Who's Afraid of Virginia Woolf?* and Ibsen's *Little Eyolf.*

Plotinsky, Melvin L. "The Transformations of Understanding: Edward Albee in the Theater of the Irresolute." *Drama Survey*, 4 (Winter 1965), 220-32. Finds the major fault of *Who's Afraid of Virginia Woolf?* to be the failure of the play's resolution in the exorcism of the child to solve the essential thematic problem of the play - the lack of communication.

Roy, Emil. "*Who's Afraid of Virginia Woolf?* and the Tradition." *Bucknell Review*, 13 (March 1965), 27-36. An excellent study which identifies Albee with the major figures of the American theater and finds in his work the tradition of the synthesis of **themes** and artistry of those artists. "This merger of divergent **conventions** into a brilliant, coherent work of art seems to be a peculiar distinction of American drama at its best." Roy correctly predicts a period of experimentation in Albee's career.

Rule, Margaret W. "An Edward Albee Bibliography." *Twentieth Century Literature*, 14 (April 1968), 35-44. Along with Richard E. Amacher, Mrs. Rule is preparing an inclusive bibliography of Albee criticism at home and abroad, scheduled for early publication by AMS Press of New York.

Rutenberg, Michael E. *Edward Albee: Playwright in Protest*. New York: Drama Book Specialists, 1969. A comprehensive study which is enriched by the author's experience as a director. He provides insights into dramatic interpretation and production techniques. The best chapter of the study is his discussion of *Box-Mao-Box* and its function as a crucial example of the New Theater.

Taylor, Marion A. "Edward Albee and August Strindberg: Some Parallels Between *The Dance of Death* and *Who's Afraid of Virginia Woolf?*" *Papers on English Language and Literature*, 1 (1965), 59-71. Another attempt to identify influences on Albee's work.

_____. "A Note on Strindberg's *The Dance of Death* and *Who's Afraid of Virginia Woolf?*" *PELL*, 2, 187-88.

Trilling, Diana. "The Riddle of Albee's *Who's Afraid of Virginia Woolf?*" *Claremont Essays*. New York: Harcourt, Brace and World, Inc., 1964, 203-27. An excellent essay which has proved influential in subsequent Albee study.

Vos, Nelvin. *Eugene Ionesco and Edward Albee: A Critical Essay.* Grand Rapids, Michigan: Eerdmans.

Welwarth, George E. *The Theater of Protest and Paradox: Developments in the Avant-Garde Drama.* New York: New York University Press, revised edition, 1971. A good general discussion of Albee's work as part of the general movement of the contemporary theater.

www.ingramcontent.com/pod-product-compliance
Lightning Source LLC
LaVergne TN
LVHW011716060526
838200LV00051B/2912